The
Eclectic
Gourmet
Guide to
San Diego

Also available from MENASHA RIDGE PRESS

The Eclectic Gourmet Guide to Los Angeles,
  by Colleen Dunn Bates

The Eclectic Gourmet Guide to New Orleans,
  by Tom Fitzmorris

The Eclectic Gourmet Guide to San Francisco & the Bay Area,
  by Richard Sterling

The Eclectic Gourmet Guide to

San Diego

Stephen Silverman

MENASHA
RIDGE
PRESS

Every effort has been made to ensure the accuracy of information throughout this book. Bear in mind, however, that prices, schedules, etc., are constantly changing. Readers should always verify information before making final plans.

Menasha Ridge Press, Inc.
P.O. Box 43059
Birmingham, Alabama 35243

Cover and text design by Suzanne Holt

Cover art by Michele Natale

ISBN 0-89732-230-4

Library of Congress Catalog Card Number: 96-49777

Manufactured in the United States of America

10 9 8 7 6 5 4 3 2 1

First Edition

CONTENTS

acknowledgments

Unless you live with a restaurant critic, you might think their lives are simple and sweet, filled with little but veal and sorbet, submissive waiters, and free lunches. Reality, unfortunately, is a wee bit different.

Reviewing restaurants anonymously—as I did for the *Eclectic Gourmet Guide*—I experience arrogant waiters, tables by the kitchen, and free lunches only by accident. That happened when I complained about a really unsatisfactory dish and an enlightened manager adjusted the bill.

Along the way, of course, there were indeed wonderful veal chops, exotic dim sum, sensational moles, seductive burritos, and stunning dessert plates.

None of it, however, could happen so pleasurably if it weren't for the four people who eat with me most often, who never order the same dish as anyone else at the table, and whose tastes are as diverse and views as articulate as any professional food reviewer.

To my wife, June, I offer a deep and abiding thanks for her energy, insight, and insistence that we try one more dish; to my daughter Morgan, for helping me understand and seek out the best of vegetarianism; to my son Brian, for unhesitatingly ordering rich and caloric items from any menu that appeals to him; and to my son Eric, for leading us all down the path of fat-free eating—though none of us could even approach his orthodoxy. These four are my greatest source of nourishment.

about the author

Stephen Silverman is a restaurant critic and food writer who has made
his home in California for more than 30 years. He spent a decade
wining and dining in San Francisco before forsaking the Bay Area in
favor of the more salubrious climes of San Diego. For the last decade, his
restaurant reviews and commentaries on food and cooking have been
heard weekly on KPBS Radio. For the last six years, his articles and
restaurant reviews have appeared monthly in *San Diego Home/Garden*
magazine.

The
Eclectic
Gourmet
Guide to
San Diego

GETTING IT RIGHT

A lot of thought went into this guide. While producing a dining guide may appear to be a straightforward endeavor, I can assure you that it is fraught with peril. I have read dining guides by authors who turn up their noses at anything except four-star French restaurants (of which there are a whole lot fewer than people think). Likewise, I have seen a guide that totally omits Thai and Indian restaurants—among others—because the author did not understand those cuisines. I have read guides absolutely devoid of criticism, written by "experts" unwilling to risk offending the source of their free meals. Finally, I've seen those books that are based on surveys and write-ins from diners whose credentials for evaluating fine dining are mysterious at best and questionable at least.

How, then, do you go about developing a truly excellent dining guide? What is the best way to get it right?

If dining guides are among the most idiosyncratic of reference books, it is primarily because the background, taste, integrity, and personal agenda of each author are problematical. The authors of most dining guides are vocational or avocational restaurant or food critics. Some of these critics are schooled professionals, with palates refined by years of practical experience and culinary study; others are journalists, often with no background in food criticism or cooking, who are arbitrarily assigned the job of reviewing restaurants by their newspaper or magazine publisher. (Although it *is* occasionally possible to find journalists who are also culinary professionals.) The worst cases are the legions of self-proclaimed food critics who mooch their way from restaurant to restaurant, growing fat on free meals in exchange for writing glowing reviews.

1

Ignorance of ethnic cuisine or old assumptions about what makes for haute cuisine particularly plague authors in cities without much ethnic variety in restaurants, or authors who have been writing for years about the same old, white linen, expense-account tourist traps. Many years ago in Lexington, Kentucky, for example, there was only one Chinese restaurant in town and it was wildly successful—in spite of the fact that it was Chinese in name only. Its specialty dishes, which were essentially American vegetable casseroles smothered in corn starch, were happily gobbled up by loyal patrons who had never been exposed to real Chinese cooking. The food was not bad, but it was not Chinese either. Visitors from out of town, inquiring about a good local Chinese restaurant, were invariably directed to this place. As you would expect, they were routinely horrified by the fare.

And, while you might argue that American diners are more sophisticated and knowledgeable nowadays than at the time of the Lexington pavilion, the evidence suggests otherwise. In Las Vegas, for instance, a good restaurant town with a number of excellent Italian eateries, the local Olive Garden (a chain restaurant) is consistently voted the city's best Italian restaurant in a yearly newspaper poll. There is absolutely nothing wrong with the Las Vegas Olive Garden, but to suggest that it is the best Italian restaurant in the city is ludicrous. In point of fact, the annual survey says much more about the relative sophistication of Las Vegas diners than it does about the quality of local Italian restaurants.

But if you pick up a guide that reflects the views of many survey respondents, a *vox populi* or reader's choice compendium, that is exactly the problem. You are dependent upon the average restaurant-goer's capacity to make sound, qualitative judgments—judgments almost always impaired by extraneous variables. How many times have you had a wonderful experience at a restaurant, only to be disappointed on a subsequent visit? Trying to reconcile the inconsistency, you recall that on your previous visit, you were in the company of someone particularly stimulating, and that perhaps you had enjoyed a couple of drinks before eating. What I am getting at is that our reflections on restaurant experiences are often colored by variables having little or nothing to do with the restaurant itself. And while I am given to the democratic process in theory, I have my doubts about depending entirely on survey forms that reflect such experiences.

There are more pragmatic arguments to be made about such eaters' guides as well. If you cannot control or properly qualify your survey respondents, you cannot assure their independence, knowledge, or critical sensitivity. And, since literally anyone can participate in such surveys, the ratings can be easily slanted by those with vested interests. How many bogus responses would it take to dramatically upgrade a restaurant's rating in a survey-based, big-city dining guide? Forty or even fewer. Why? Because the publisher receives patron reports (survey responses, readers' calls) covering more restaurants than can be listed in the book. Thus the "voting" is distributed over such a large number of candidate restaurants that the median number of reports for the vast majority of establishments is 120 or fewer. A cunning restaurant proprietor who is willing to stuff the ballot box, therefore, could easily improve his own rating—or lower that of a competitor.

So my mission in the *Eclectic Gourmet Guides* is to provide you with the most meaningful, useful, and accessible restaurant evaluations possible. Weighing the alternatives, I have elected to work with culinary experts, augmenting their opinions with a carefully qualified survey population of totally independent local diners of demonstrated culinary sophistication. The experts I have sought to author the *Eclectic Gourmet Guides* are knowledgeable, seasoned professionals; they have studied around the world, written cookbooks or columns, and closely followed the development of restaurants in their cities. They are well versed in ethnic dining, many having studied cuisines in their native lands. And they have no prejudice about high or low cuisine. They are as at home in a Tupelo, Mississippi, catfish shack as in an exclusive French restaurant on New York's Upper East Side. Thus the name "Eclectic Gourmet."

Equally important, I have sought experts who make every effort to conduct their reviews anonymously, and who always pay full menu prices for their meals. We are credible not only because we are knowledgeable, but also because we are independent.

You, the reader of this *Eclectic Gourmet Guide,* are the inspiration for and, we hope, the beneficiary of our diligence and methodology. Though we cannot evaluate your credentials as a restaurant critic, your opinion as a consumer—of this guide and the restaurants within—is very important to us. A clip-out survey can be found at the back of the book; please tell us about your dining experiences and let us know whether you agree with our reviews.

Eat well. Be happy.

Bob Sehlinger

dining in san diego

exploring the corner pocket

Over the last several decades, San Diego's cosmopolitan character has soared. That means if you poke around in this southwesternmost pocket of America, you'll discover food as glorious as any in the nation. Not only that, you'll find abundant variety, great character, and enough edge to confirm the fact that you're hovering on the Pacific Rim.

Given San Diego's location, it's to be expected that the local restaurant business is strongly effected by large Asian, Central, and South American populations. That's indisputable. But San Diego is also exposed to the same food trends that visit other parts of the country. We've weathered Thai, Southwestern, Cajun, Fusion, Italian, East Indian, and now Steakhouse. Some restaurants featuring these foods were just passing through, but a good number seem tethered for the long haul. Even so, as one fades out there's always another anxious to replace it.

In part, it's the combination of location, immigration, and rising sophistication that helps mark San Diego as an enormous tureen of flavors. But there's much that's unexpected too.

local surprises

Fast-food restaurants are found in abundance throughout San Diego. In order to distinguish themselves from an overcrowded and intensely competitive field, some purveyors work hard to overcome the traditional handicap of rotating cooks and half-hearted management. Therefore they've devised unusual dishes that can survive roughneck preparation and, voila!, the result is often superb fast food. Perhaps it's a dubious distinction, but San Diego may have some of the best fast food in the nation. That's an important tenet to remember, and so is this principle: Don't hate it just because it's fast.

Though it is no surprise that the Mexican influence is very strong in San Diego, Mexican food is not nearly as evolved as you'd expect in a city where the number of border crossings is the highest in the world. Mass-merchandized Mexican is everywhere, and it's so fully acculturated that even in the Hispanic parts of town food can be as dreary as at a roadside Taco Bell. The most interesting Mexican food is found primarily in small, decidedly regional restaurants.

A quirk in the Mexican food industry has also been a source of local amusement for more than a decade. It's called the 'Berto phenomenon, and it began years ago with Roberto's, an expanding chain of Mexican fast-food places where the staples were tacos, burritos, enchiladas, and other garden variety foods which were known to be both filling and cheap. Roberto's success spawned a series of not-so-subtle imitators. They called themselves Aiberto's, Alberto's, Aliberto's, Hilberto's, Jilberto's, Loberto's, etc. through the alphabet. At last count there were more than 30 different 'Bertos, all serving approximately the same food, but prepared with varying degrees of sanitation.

One of the wonders of San Diego is the paucity of superb fish restaurants. A casual glance at a list of restaurants might suggest there are many, but a significant number are old-school eateries where fish is considered edible only if its filleted, breaded, and fried, à la the Mrs. Paul school of fish deconstruction. Good seafood restaurants number no more than half a dozen, and some are found in very unlikely places.

value is a state of mind

Notwithstanding the local variety and opportunity, San Diegans retain some quirkiness about food.

Ever since the late 1880s, when modern San Diego first got started, most of the longtime residents have been steadfast in their devotion to comfort food. Comfort food starts at home, of course, and home is still where many locals prefer their dining.

That reality plays against the fact that San Diego is the sixth-largest city in the nation and its population spirals to well over a million. Restaurants number in the thousands. Obviously, not *everybody* stays home to eat. Yet when San Diegans go out for dinner, they take their values with them. The result is that San Diego is still firmly rooted in the great middle ground of taste: San Diegans most enjoy what's simple, good, and moderately priced.

This emphasis on simplicity, goodness, and price has come to define the vast center of the local restaurant business. It's like a great fried egg whose golden yolk occupies 90% of the surface. Within the sunshiny central puddle are terrific eating experiences. Lots are mom-and-pop shops, lots are family run, and lots make a point, even a virtue, of not being too fancy. But it's along the slender white perimeter where the fine restaurants attempt to dig in. Most are never permitted to forget they're on the edge, along the outer banks of popularity. As a consequence, it's no secret that San Diego has difficulty supporting high-quality, high-end restaurants. Hotels, the central business district, and neighborhoods throughout the county are strewn with the bones of great gustatory experiences that received high praise but few patrons.

food geography

Because San Diego County is large enough to be a nation-state, restaurants are scattered like so much buckshot. The greatest number are in the urban and suburban neighborhoods, but their frequency swells in a few areas downtown and along the coast. The most significant concentration occurs in the Gaslamp District, a historic area downtown just east of the modern landmark that is the Horton Plaza shopping center. After decades of preening, pump-priming, and redevelopment funding, the Gaslamp has finally (though not entirely) emerged from its unpolished skid-row cocoon as an exhilarated adolescent. What's odd is that the Gaslamp is also the center of the Italian restaurant industry in San Diego, with several dozen *trattorias* and *ristorantes* located within a four-minute walk of one another. That's a considerably greater number than you'll find in the Little Italy section of town.

Go inland five or ten miles and, though still within city limits, you'll also find yourself in one of several immigrant community concentrations. The Chinese restaurants that once dominated the eastern stretches of University Avenue are increasingly supplanted by small Laotian, Thai, Korean, Cambodian, and Vietnamese places. Though most cater predominantly to natives and may be distinguished by shifting staffs and ownerships, there is a form of graduation that occurs with a relocation to the Convoy Street area.

Convoy Street is a hallucination of urban planning, where strip malls are chockablock as a river of Jelly Bellys, and where finding any *one* destination among the entangled paint stores, markets, car dealerships, donut houses, fabric outlets, and hundreds of restaurants is an awesome challenge. Yet it is also the East-West meeting ground, a place to "make it" that's away from ethnic neighborhoods and poorly lit streets. Along Convoy Street and its environs are superb Asian restaurants whose clientele are a mix of suburban and ethnic diners and are themselves places of crossing cultures.

Another major concentration of restaurants is found along the coast, sometimes in linear arrangements that mimic the continental edge, and sometimes in clusters that radiate inland and fuse to a community. In areas like La Jolla—as resplendent a dining cluster as you'll find along the Southern California coast—there is no embarrassment at the accumulated riches, but instead an expectation of culinary and visual splendor. A small but regular turnover in restaurants suggests that either the expectations or the rents are too high for some, but a surprising majority endure. Moreover, geography remains blessedly dependable and spectacular waterfront views are *almost* commonplace.

Further north, in cities like Encinitas and Solana Beach, the concentration of restaurants feathers out and neighborhood history washes in. Though virtually all the coastal communities have succeeded at upscaling themselves, more than just a remnant of the 60s remains. A significant portion of coastal locals are seriously dedicated to simplification, surfing, and funky-business. In communities where expensive homes spring up next to summer cottages, expect a similar muddle and diversity among the restaurants.

dRESSiNG THE pART

Except for a few places, restaurant dining in San Diego tends to be casual. That is, of course, distinctly different from flip-flops, T-shirt, and shorts dining. If you look "Dressy Casual," a recommendation you'll find suggested often in this guide, you can go almost anywhere. And if in your travels you happen to come across a restaurant that seems full of people in very casual dress who seem to be having too much of a good time, go in and join them. Don't be put off because the place looks like its full of tourists; that *is* what locals look like too.

TOURIST MAGNETS

There are some must-do restaurants visitors hear about before they arrive in San Diego, and some places that tourist magazines tout as "Not-to-Miss." Recommendations from tourist magazines are usually more suspect than advice from friends. Keep in mind that more than a few local restaurants live off reputations made a decade ago that have been unjustified ever since. So when was the last time your friends ate in San Diego?

Unfortunately, some of the least appetizing food in town happens to be available at two of the most worthwhile visitor stops, the San Diego Zoo (its northerly companion is the Wild Animal Park) and Sea World. We all have to take it on faith that more attention is paid to the animal food than the human version. At the Zoo, the single option is the attractive, moderately priced restaurant called Albert's, which is named after a much-loved and now deceased gorilla. Albert's appeal is more to adults than kids. Otherwise, you're better off taking a picnic lunch or just snacking at the Zoo / Wild Animal Park and Sea World. Eat before or after your visit.

San Diego has its own local chapter of Planet Hollywood (Horton Plaza, 702-7827) and the Hard Rock Cafe (La Jolla, 454-5101). In both places, the hype, setting, and sound level overwhelm culinary concerns. We also have an outpost of the Texas-based Dick's Last Resort, which is in the Gaslamp and noted in this guide more for its clever advertising and rowdy excessiveness than its vittles. National and California-based chain restaurants are well represented locally. But given the many dining options, you might want to wait until you've been everyplace else before venturing in to the Olive Garden, Chevy's, and California Pizza Kitchen (CPK), all of which have multiple units in and around San Diego.

Several of the places tourist brochures celebrate—which you'll also find in the pages of this guide—include a number of restaurants in Old Town such as Casa di Bandini and Old Town Mexican Cafe. Both are worthwhile. In fact, when you visit Old Town State Park, you'll find a number of outdoor restaurants that are so charming it's difficult to resist stopping for lunch. Stay and indulge. The setting alone makes lunch worthwhile. Outside of Old Town, some perennial visitor favorites are the Corvette Diner (see guide), Jake's Del Mar (see guide), and Bully's (Mission Valley, (619) 291-2665; La Jolla, (619) 459-2768; Del Mar, (619) 755-1660). At Bully's, the emphasis is on steak, potatoes, brew, and very low lighting.

NEWCOMERS

Some newer restaurants in town have developed a following:

Baja Brewing Company
203 Fifth Avenue
Downtown   (619) 231-6667
Mexican/Southwestern food in a large converted warehouse, with home-brewed beers.

Bird Rock Cafe
5656 La Jolla Boulevard
La Jolla   (619) 551-4090
It's American food in a neighborhood setting, but with lots of flavorful twists.

Blue Point Coastal Cuisine
565 Fifth Avenue
Downtown   (619) 233-6623
It's got the ambience of a sophisticated 1950s supper club, but the patrons are often casually dressed. Seafood fills the menu.

Kensington Grill
4055 Adams Avenue
Central   (619) 281-4014
Well off the beaten track, this local eatery has high aspirations, earnestness, and an inventive menu.

Kimo Sabe
3958 Fifth Avenue
Uptown   (619) 220-6802
Pacific Rim influences cast into a Southwestern mold. Virtually every dish requires an explantion from your server.

Mimi's Cafe

5180 Mission Center Road
Mission Valley   (619) 491-0284

This is a cozy, upscale, and very American coffee shop, with so much frilly decor that Mary Poppins might feel claustrophobic.

Portobello

714 Fourth Avenue
Downtown   (619) 232-4440

A larger, sweller version of the cramped Panevino (see restaurant profile), this brand new trattoria is operated by the same owners and literally connects with Panevino in the rear. There's a cigar bar near the front door.

Primadonna

2151 Avenida de la Playa
La Jolla   (619) 551-1221

Comfortable and unpretentious neighborhood Italian restaurant with many low-fat menu choices. The narrow sidewalk dining area fills fast.

bEST bETS*

◆ Best Bagels

Baltimore Bagel / Einstein's Bagels

They're all over town; check the phone book for the location closest to you.

◆ Best Bread

Solunto Baking Company

1643 India Street, Downtown   (619) 233-3506

Bread & Cie

350 University Avenue, Downtown   (619) 683-9322

San Diego Artisan Bakery

1551 Escondido Boulevard, Escondido   (619) 740-5963

*The restaurants recommended below are profiled alphabetically, starting on page 51, unless otherwise noted.

Best Chicken Soup

El Tecolote
6110 Friars Road, Mission Valley   (619) 295-2087

Best Delis

D.Z. Aiken's
Alvarado Plaza, 6930 Alvarado Road, San Diego East
   (619) 265-0218
Milton's
2660 Via de la Valle, Del Mar   (619) 792-2225

Best Desserts

Extraordinary Desserts
2829 Fifth Avenue, Downtown   (619) 294-7001
Kemo Sabe
3958 University Avenue, Uptown   (619) 220-6802

Best Grilled Chicken

Saffron
3731 India Street, Downtown   (619) 574-0177

Best Healthy Dining

Souplantation
17210 Bernardo Center Drive, Rancho Bernardo, North County
   (619) 675-3353
9158 Fletcher Parkway, San Diego East   (619) 462-4232
1860 Marron Road, North County   (619) 434-9100
Daily's Fit and Fresh
8915 Towne Center Drive, Mission Valley   (619) 453-1112

Best Hot Dog

Price Club
It's their Hebrew National hot dogs, available ready-to-eat at stands
   outside the stores. Many locations; check the phone book for the
   location nearest you.

Best Pizza

Aladdin Mediterranean Cafe
5420 Clairemont Mesa Boulevard, Mission Valley   (619) 573-0000
Sammy's California Woodfired Pizza
702 Pearl Street, La Jolla   (619) 456-5222
12925 El Camino Road, Del Mar   (619) 259-6600
770 4th Avenue, Downtown   (619) 230-8888

Best Places to Take Adolescents

Corvette Diner, Bar & Grill
3946 Fifth Avenue, Downtown   (619) 542-1001
Hard Rock Cafe
909 Prospect Street, La Jolla   (619) 454-5101
Planet Hollywood
179 Horton Plaza, Downtown   (619) 702-7827

Best Place to Think about Running Away from It All

Sally's
Hyatt Regency Hotel, One Market Place, Downtown
    (619) 687-6080
At an outside table on the esplanade at lunchtime with the sun shining and the boats bobbing, you can't help but be carried away.

Best Shrimp Burrito

Fins
15817 Bernardo Center Drive, Suite 104, North County
    (619) 484-FINS
9460H Mira Mesa Boulevard, Mission Valley   (619) 549-FINS
8657 Villa La Jolla Drive, #103, La Jolla   (619) 270-FINS
1640 Camino Del Rio North, Mission Valley Center
    (619) 283-FINS

Best Sushi Bars

Cafe Japengo
8960 University Center Lane, Mission Valley   (619) 450-3355
Katsu Seafood and Steakhouse
1020 West San Marcos Boulevard, San Marcos   (619) 744-7156
Sushi Ota
4529 Mission Bay Drive, Mission Bay   (619) 270-5670

- Best Tortilla Chips

  El Indio
  3695 India Street, Downtown   (619) 299-0333
  409 F Street, Downtown   (619) 239-8151
  4120 Mission Boulevard, Mission Bay   (619) 272-8226

- Best View with Breakfast

  Pannikin's Brockton Villa
  1235 Coast Boulevard, La Jolla   (619) 454-7393

- Best View with Lunch

  George's Cafe and Ocean Terrace
  1250 Prospect Street, La Jolla   (619) 454-4244

- Best View with Dinner

  Azzura Point
  Loews Coronado Bay Resort, 4000 Coronado Bay Road,
      Coronado   (619) 424-4000
  Epazote
  Del Mar Plaza, 1555 Camino Del Mar, Del Mar   (619) 259-9966
  Il Fornaio Cucina Italiana
  Del Mar Plaza, 1555 Camino Del Mar, Del Mar   (619) 755-8876
  Jake's Del Mar
  1660 Coast Boulevard, Del Mar   (619) 755-2002
  530 Marina Boulevard, Chula Vista   (619) 476-0400
  Pacifica Del Mar
  Del Mar Plaza, 1555 Camino Del Mar, Del Mar   (619) 792-0476
  Top o' the Cove
  1216 Prospect Street, La Jolla   (619) 454-7779
  Top of the Market
  In The Fish Market, 750 North Harbor Drive, Downtown
      (619) 232-3474

- Best View with a Drink

  Enoteca Fornaio
  Del Mar Plaza, 1555 Camino del Mar, Del Mar   (619) 755-8876
  Marine Room Restaurant
  La Jolla Beach and Tennis Club, 2000 Spindrift Drive, La Jolla
      (619) 459-7222

Mister A's
2550 Fifth Avenue, Downtown   (619) 239-1377
Top of the Hyatt
Hyatt Regency San Diego, One Market Place, Downtown
    (619) 232-1234

- ◆ Best Wine Lists

El Bizcocho
Rancho Bernardo Inn, 17550 Bernardo Oaks Drive,
    North County   (619) 487-1611
Elario's
7955 La Jolla Shores Drive, La Jolla   (619) 459-0541
Top o' the Cove
1216 Prospect Street, La Jolla   (619) 454-7779
WineSellar and Brasserie
9550 Waples Street, Suite 115, Mission Valley   (619) 450-9576

- ◆ Best Wine Dinners

El Bizcocho
Rancho Bernardo Inn, 17550 Bernardo Oaks Drive,
    North County   (619) 487-1611

RECOMMENDATIONS FOR SPECIAL PURPOSE DINING*

- ◆ Business Dining

Belgian Lion
2265 Bacon Street, Mission Bay   (619) 223-2700
California Cuisine
1027 University Avenue, Downtown   (619) 543-0790
Dobson's
956 Broadway Circle, Downtown   (619) 231-6771
El Bizcocho
Rancho Bernardo Inn, 17550 Bernardo Oaks Drive,
    North County   (619) 487-1611
Laurel
505 Laurel Street, Downtown   (619) 239-2222

*The restaurants recommended below are profiled alphabetically, starting on page
51, unless otherwise noted.

Montanas American Grill
1421 University Avenue, Downtown   (619) 297-0722
Prego
1370 Frazee Road, Mission Valley   (619) 294-4700
Rainwater's
1202 Kettner Boulevard, Downtown   (619) 233-5757

◆ Quiet and Romantic Dining

These are the places where marriage and other more temporary proposals are common as a plate du jour.

Grant Grill
U.S. Grant Hotel, 326 Broadway, Downtown   (619) 232-3121
Mille Fleur
6009 Paseo Delicias, Rancho Sante Fe, North County Coastal
    (619) 756-3085
Prince of Wales Grill
Hotel Del Coronado, 1500 Orange Avenue, Coronado
    (619) 522-8818
Rancho Valencia Restaurant
5921 Valencia Circle, Rancho Sante Fe, North County Coastal
    (619) 756-3645
Thee Bungalow
4996 West Point Loma Boulevard, Mission Bay   (619) 224-2884
Top o' the Cove
1216 Prospect Street, La Jolla   (619) 454-7779

◆ Late Night Dining

San Diego is not much of a late night town, so "late" is used here to mean you can order dinner after 10:30 or 11 P.M., primarily on weekends. The rest of the week you'll need to call to find out the hours.

Cafe Sevilla
555 Fourth Avenue, Downtown   (619) 233-5979

City Deli
535 University Avenue, Uptown   (619) 295-2747
Crest Cafe
425 Robinson Avenue, Downtown   (619) 295-2510
Croce's Restaurant
802 Fifth Avenue, Downtown   (619) 233-4355

Dick's Last Resort
345 Fourth Avenue, Downtown   (619) 231-9100
Fio's
801 Fifth Avenue, Downtown   (619) 234-3467
Greek Town Taverna
431 E Street, Downtown   (619) 232-0461
La Strada
702 Fifth Avenue, Downtown   (619) 239-3400
La Terrazza
8008 Girare Avenue, La Jolla   (619) 459-9750
Ole Madrid
755 Fifth Avenue, Downtown   (619) 557-0416
Panevino
722 Fifth Avenue, Downtown   (619) 595-7959
Prego
1370 Frazee Road, Mission Valley   (619) 294-4700
Rainwater's
1202 Kettner Boulevard, Downtown   (619) 233-5757
Saska's
3768 Mission Boulevard, Mission Beach   (619) 488-7311

perfect day

If you've only got one or two days in San Diego and you only want to eat where you'll get very good food and distinctly local character, focus on the places below. Sure it means going whole hog. But if you spend one glorious day having breakfast, lunch, and dinner from the restaurants on this list, you'll end your day bursting with pleasure.

+ Breakfast

  Cafe 222   Downtown
  Pannikin's Brockton Villa   La Jolla
  Zinc's   North County Coastal

+ Lunch

  Aladdin   Central
  Chilango's   Uptown

Daily's La Jolla
Fins La Jolla, Kearny Mesa, and North County Inland
George's Ocean Terrace La Jolla

+ Dinner

Azzura Point Coronado
Marius Coronado

understanding the ratings

We have developed detailed profiles for the best restaurants (in our opinion) in town. Each profile features an easily scanned heading that allows you, in just a second, to check out the restaurant's name, cuisine, star rating, cost, quality rating, and value rating.

Star Rating. The star rating is an overall rating that encompasses the entire dining experience, including style, service, and ambience in addition to the taste, presentation, and quality of the food. Five stars is the highest rating possible and connotes the best of everything. Four-star restaurants are exceptional and three-star restaurants are well above average. Two-star restaurants are good. One star is used to connote an average restaurant that demonstrates an unusual capability in some area of specialization, for example, an otherwise unmemorable place that has great barbecued chicken.

Cost. Below the star rating is an expense description that provides a comparative sense of how much a complete meal will cost. A complete meal for our purposes consists of an entree with vegetable or side dish, and choice of soup or salad. Appetizers, desserts, drinks, and tips are excluded.

Inexpensive	$14 or less per person
Moderate	$15–25 per person
Expensive	$26–39 per person
Very Expensive	$40 or more per person

Quality Rating.   Below the cost rating appear a number and a letter. The number is a quality rating based on a scale of 0–100, with 100 being the highest (best) rating attainable. The quality rating is based expressly on the taste, freshness of ingredients, preparation, presentation, and creativity of food served. There is no consideration of price. If you are a person who wants the best food available, and cost is not an issue, you need look no further than the quality ratings.

Value Rating.   If, on the other hand, you are looking for both quality and value, then you should check the value rating, expressed in letters. The value ratings are defined as follows:

A   Exceptional value, a real bargain
B   Good value
C   Fair value, you get exactly what you pay for
D   Somewhat overpriced
F   Significantly overpriced

locating the restaurant

Just below the restaurant name is a designation for geographic zone. This zone description will give you a general idea of where the restaurant described is located. For ease of use, we divide San Diego into 8 geographic zones.

Zone 1.   North County Inland
Zone 2.   North County Coastal
Zone 3.   La Jolla
Zone 4.   Mission Valley and the Mesas
Zone 5.   Mission Bay and Beaches
Zone 6.   Downtown / Uptown / Central
Zone 7.   San Diego East / East County
Zone 8.   Coronado / South Bay / Tijuana

If you are downtown and intend to walk or take a cab to dinner, you may want to choose a restaurant from among those located in Zone 6. If you have a car, you might include restaurants from contiguous zones in your consideration.

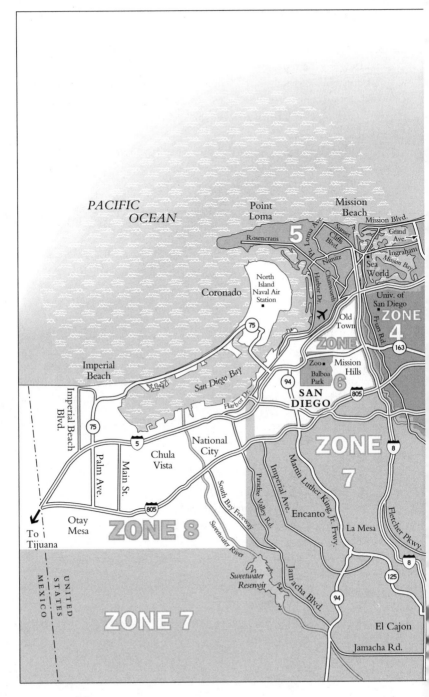

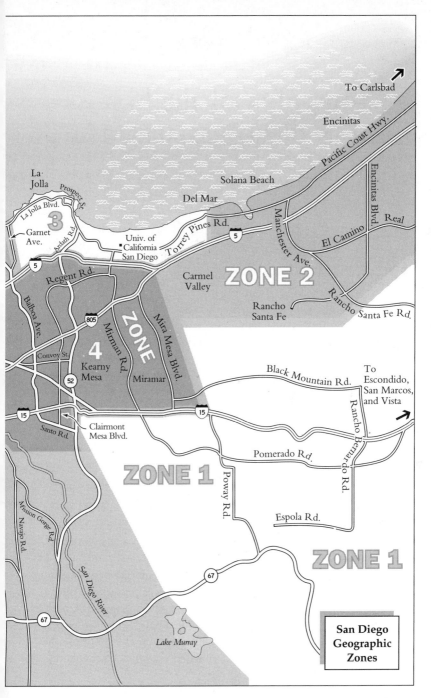

To Carlsbad

Encinitas

Pacific Coast Hwy.

La Jolla

Prospect St.

Solana Beach

Del Mar

Encinitas Blvd.

Real

La Jolla Blvd.

3

Garnet Ave.

Ardath Rd.

Torrey Pines Rd.

Univ. of California San Diego

5

Manchester Ave.

El Camino

ZONE 2

5

Regent Rd.

Carmel Valley

Rancho Santa Fe Rd.

Balboa Ave.

805

ZONE

Mirman Rd.

Mira Mesa Blvd.

Rancho Santa Fe

Convoy St.

4

Kearny Mesa

Miramar

Black Mountain Rd.

To Escondido, San Marcos, and Vista

52

15

Clairmont Mesa Blvd.

15

Santo Rd.

Rancho Bernardo Rd.

Pomerado Rd.

ZONE 1

Mission Gorge Rd.

Navajo Rd.

Poway Rd.

Espola Rd.

ZONE 1

San Diego River

67

ZONE 1

67

Lake Murray

San Diego Geographic Zones

21

OUR pick of THE bEST SAN diEGO RESTAURANTS

Because restaurants are opening and closing all the time in San Diego, we have tried to confine our list to establishments—or chefs—with a proven track record over a fairly long period of time. Those newer or changed establishments that demonstrate staying power and consistency will be profiled in subsequent editions.

The list is highly selective. Non-inclusion of a particular place does not necessarily indicate that the restaurant is not good, but only that it was not ranked among the best or most consistent in its genre. Detailed profiles of each restaurant follow in alphabetical order at the end of this chapter.

A NOTE AboUT SpElliNG

Most diners who enjoy ethnic restaurants have noticed subtle variations in the spelling of certain dishes and preparations from one menu to the next. A noodle dish found on almost all Thai menus, for example, appears in one restaurant as *pad thai,* in another as *Phat Thai,* and in a third as *Phad Thai.*

This and similar inconsistencies arise from attempts to derive a phonetic English spelling from the name of a dish as pronounced in its country of origin. While one particular English spelling might be more frequently used than others, there is usually no definitive correct spelling for the names of many dishes. In this guide, we have elected to use the spelling most commonly found in authoritative ethnic cookbooks and other reference works.

We call this to your attention because the spelling we use in this guide could be different from that which you encounter on the menu in a certain restaurant. We might say, for instance, that the *tabbouleh* is good at the Pillars of Lebanon, while at the restaurant itself the dish is listed on the menu as *tabouli*.

Restaurants by Cuisine

Name	Star Rating	Price Rating	Quality Rating	Value Rating	Zone
Afghani					
Khyber Pass	★★★	Inexp/Mod	82	C	4
American					
University Club	★★★★	Mod/Exp	94	C	6
Laurel	★★★★	Moderate	93	B	6
Montanas American Grill	★★★★	Inexp/Mod	93	B	6
Prince of Wales Grill	★★★★	Expensive	90	C	8
Rainwater's on Kettner	★★★★	Mod/Exp	90	D	6
Souplantation	★★★★	Inexpensive	90	A	1,2,4,5,7
Islands	★★★	Inexpensive	88	B	1,4
Zinc Cafe	★★★	Inexpensive	88	C	2
Claim Jumper	★★★	Inexp/Mod	85	A	1,2,7
Hops! Bistro & Brewery	★★★	Inexpensive	85	B	4,6
Rhinoceros Cafe and Grill	★★★	Inexp/Mod	85	B	8
George's Cafe and Ocean Terrace	★★★	Moderate	84	C	3
Oscar's	★★★	Inexpensive	81	B	1,2,4
Cafe on Park	★★★	Inexpensive	80	B	6
The Corvette Diner, Bar & Grill	★★	Inexpensive	79	C	6
Cheese Shop	★★	Inexpensive	78	C	3,6
Galaxy Grill	★★	Inexpensive	76	B	6
Big Kitchen Cafe	★★	Inexpensive	75	B	6
Crest Cafe	★★	Inexpensive	75	C	6
Harry's Cafe Gallery	★★	Inexpensive	75	C	3
Jake's Del Mar	★★	Moderate	75	C	2,8
Adam's Steak and Eggs	★★	Inexpensive	74	B	4
Le Peep	★★	Inexpensive	73	B	1,2
Allen's Alley	★★	Inexpensive	70	B	1
Hob Nob Hill	★	Inexp/Mod	75	B	6
Dick's Last Resort	★	Inexp/Mod	68	C	6
Bakery Cafe					
Bread & Cie	★★★★	Inexpensive	90	B	6
Bakery Lafayette	★★★	Inexpensive	84	B	1

Name	Star Rating	Price Rating	Quality Rating	Value Rating	Zone
A la Francaise	★★	Inexpensive	79	C	6
Solunto Baking Company	★★	Inexpensive	78	B	6
Barbecue					
Big Stone Lodge	★★	Inexp/Mod	78	C	1
Buffalo Joe's	★★	Inexp/Mod	72	C	6
California					
Azzura Point	★★★★★	Expensive	98	B	8
California Cuisine	★★★★	Moderate	92	B	6
George's at the Cove	★★★★	Mod/Exp	92	C	3
Croce's Restaurant	★★★★	Moderate	90	B	6
Daily's Fit and Fresh	★★★★	Inexpensive	90	B	4
Pannikin's Brockton Villa	★★★	Inexp/Mod	89	B	3
150 Grand Cafe	★★★	Inexp/Mod	80	C	1
Fifth & Hawthorn	★★	Moderate	79	C	6
Cafe 222	★★	Inexpensive	78	C	6
California French					
Rancho Valencia Restaurant	★★★★★	Exp/Very Exp	95	B	2
Cindy Black's	★★★	Moderate	88	C	3
Dobson's	★★★	Moderate	88	C	6
Bernard'O Restaurant	★★★	Moderate	84	C	1
Cafe Champagne	★★★	Inexp/Mod	80	C	1
Delicias	★★★	Mod/Exp	80	D	2
French Gourmet	★★★	Inexp/Mod	80	C	3, 5
Cafe Eleven	★★	Inexp/Mod	78	C	6
Chinese					
Jasmine	★★★★	Moderate	92	C	4
Emerald Chinese Restaurant	★★★	Inexp/Mod	88	C	4
Emperor's Palace	★★★	Inexpensive	80	B	1
Panda Inn	★★★	Inexp/Mod	80	C	6
Canton Seafood Restaurant	★★	Inexpensive	75	B	7
Mr. Chow's	★★	Inexpensive	72	B	4
Continental					
El Bizcocho	★★★★★	Expensive	97	C	1

Name	Star Rating	Price Rating	Quality Rating	Value Rating	Zone
Continental (continued)					
Top o' the Cove	★★★★	Expensive	93	C	3
Le Fontainebleau Room	★★★	Expensive	88	C	6
Thee Bungalow	★★★	Moderate	88	B	5
Grant Grill	★★★	Mod/Exp	85	C	6
Mister A's	★★★	Mod/Exp	80	C	6
Creole/Cajun					
Bayou Bar & Grill	★★★	Moderate	80	C	6
Cuban					
Andres' Cuban Restaurant	★★★	Inexpensive	80	B	4
Deli					
Chez Odette	★★★	Inexpensive	85	B	6
D. Z. Aiken's	★★★	Inexpensive	80	B	7
Milton's	★★★	Inexpensive	80	B	2
Desserts					
Extraordinary Desserts	★★★	Inexpensive	85	D	6
Gelato Vero Caffe	★★	Inexpensive	79	B	6
Julian Pie Co.	★★	Inexpensive	77	B	1
French					
Marius	★★★★★	Exp/Very Exp	99	B	8
Mille Fleurs	★★★★★	Exp/Very Exp	98	C	2
Belgian Lion	★★★★	Mod/Exp	93	B	5
WineSellar and Brasserie	★★★★	Mod/Exp	93	C	4
Marine Room Restaurant	★★	Mod/Exp	79	C	3
French Market Grill	★★	Moderate	78	D	1
German/American					
Karl Strauss' Old Columbia Brewery & Grill	★★★	Inexpensive	80	B	3,4,6
Greek					
Aesop's Tables	★★★	Inexp/Mod	85	B	4
Athens Market Taverna	★★★	Inexp/Mod	82	C	6

26

Name	Star Rating	Price Rating	Quality Rating	Value Rating	Zone
Indian					
Wazwan Indian Cuisine	★★★	Inexpensive	80	B	1,4
International / Vegetarian					
Monsoon	★★★	Inexpensive	82	B	6
Kung Food Vegetarian Restaurant	★★	Inexpensive	72	B	6
Italian					
Prego	★★★★	Moderate	94	C	4
Panevino	★★★★	Moderate	93	D	6
Piatti	★★★★	Moderate	92	C	3
Trattoria Acqua	★★★★	Moderate	90	C	3
Fio's	★★★	Moderate	89	C	6
Busalacchi's Ristorante	★★★	Inexp/Mod	88	B	6
La Strada	★★★	Moderate	88	C	6
Manhattan	★★★	Mod/Exp	88	C	3
Sorrentino's Ristorante Italiano	★★★	Inexp/Mod	88	B	4
Arrivederci Italian Ristorante	★★★	Inexp/Mod	85	D	6
Vigilucci's Trattoria Italiana	★★★	Inexp/Mod	85	B	2
Caldo Pomodoro	★★★	Inexp/Mod	84	B	2
Trattoria Mannino	★★★	Inexp/Mod	83	B	3
Cafe Luna	★★★	Inexp/Mod	81	B	1
Salvatore's	★★★	Moderate	81	C	6
Sfuzzi	★★★	Inexp/Mod	80	C	6
Il Fornaio Cucina Italiana / Enoteca Fornaio	★★	Moderate	79	C	2
Domenic's Ristorante	★★	Inexpensive	73	B	1
Italian / Pizza					
Sammy's California Woodfired Pizza	★★★★	Inexp/Mod	90	B	2,3,6
D'Lish Gourmet Pasta and Pizza	★★★	Inexpensive	80	B	3,8

Name	Star Rating	Price Rating	Quality Rating	Value Rating	Zone
Italian / Pizza (continued)					
Pizza Nova	★★★	Inexpensive	80	C	4,5,6
Filippi's Pizza Grotto	★★	Inexpensive	75	B	1,6,8
Japanese					
Shien of Osaka	★★★	Inexpensive	85	B	1
Ichiban	★★★	Inexpensive	80	A	5,6
Niban Japanese Restaurant	★★	Inexpensive	79	A	4
Little Tokyo	★★	Inexpensive	76	B	1,6
Japanese / Mexican					
Banzai Cantina	★★★	Inexp/Mod	82	C	6
Japanese / Sushi Bar					
Sushi Ota	★★★	Moderate	88	D	5
Sushi Deli	★★	Inexpensive	76	B	6
Latin American					
Berta's	★★★	Inexpensive	81	B	6
Mexican					
Chilango's Mexico City Grill	★★★★	Inexpensive	90	A	6
Fins	★★★	Inexpensive	89	B	1,3,4
Old Town Mexican Cafe	★★★	Inexpensive	84	B	6
El Tecolote	★★★	Inexpensive	82	B	4
Hernandez' Hideaway	★★★	Inexp/Mod	80	B	1
Palenque	★★★	Inexp/Mod	80	B	5
Carnitas Uruapan	★★	Inexpensive	79	B	8
Alfonso's	★★	Inexp/Mod	75	C	3
Rubio's	★★	Inexpensive	74	B	1,2,4,5, 6,7,8
Casa de Bandini	★★	Inexp/Mod	72	C	6
El Indio	★★	Inexpensive	72	B	5,6
Mexican / Seafood					
Los Arcos	★★★★	Inexpensive	90	A	8
La Costa	★★★	Moderate	87	B	8

Name	Star Rating	Price Rating	Quality Rating	Value Rating	Zone
Middle Eastern					
Aladdin Mediterranean Cafe	★★★	Inexpensive	89	B	4
Pacific Rim / Sushi Bar					
Cafe Japengo	★★★	Inexp / Mod	88	C	4
Peruvian					
Machupicchu	★★★	Inexpensive	80	B	5
Seafood					
Cafe Pacifica	★★★★	Moderate	94	C	6
Pacifica Del Mar	★★★★	Moderate	94	C	2
Sally's	★★★★	Mod / Exp	92	C	6
The Fish Market / Top of the Market	★★★	Mod / Exp	89	C	2,6
Anthony's Star of the Sea Room	★★★	Expensive	83	D	6
Pelly's	★★★	Inexpensive	80	B	2
Peohe's	★★★	Mod / Exp	80	D	8
Point Loma Seafoods	★★	Inexpensive	79	C	5
Humphrey's	★★	Mod / Exp	72	C	5
Anthony's Fish Grotto	★★	Inexp / Mod	70	C	1,6,7,8
Sportsmen's Seafood	★	Inexpensive	60	D	5
Southern / Cajun					
Brendory's by the Sea	★★★	Inexpensive	89	B	8
Southwestern					
Indigo Grill	★★★★	Inexp / Mod	90	A	6
Epazote	★★★	Inexp / Mod	85	C	2
Cilantro's	★★★	Inexp / Mod	84	C	2
Southwestern / Sushi Bar					
Chino	★★	Mod / Exp	79	D	6
Spanish / Mediterranean					
Ole Madrid	★★	Moderate	75	D	6

Restaurants by Cuisine (continued)

Name	Star Rating	Price Rating	Quality Rating	Value Rating	Zone
Steaks					
Ruth's Chris Steak House	★★★★	Exp/Very Exp	94	D	6
Rainwater's on Kettner	★★★★	Mod/Exp	90	D	6
Buffalo Ranch Steakhouse	★★	Inexp/Mod	78	B	I
Thai					
Saffron	★★★	Inexpensive	86	A	6
Karinya Thai Cuisine	★★★	Inexpensive	82	C	5
Old Town Thai	★★★	Inexpensive	80	B	6
Thai Chada	★★★	Inexpensive	80	B	5
Vietnamese					
Pho Pasteur	★★★	Inexpensive	80	B	4

Restaurants by Star Rating

Name	Cuisine	Price Rating	Quality Rating	Value Rating	Zone
Five-Star Restaurants					
Marius	French	Exp/Very Exp	99	B	8
Azzura Point	California/Mediterranean	Expensive	98	B	8
Mille Fleurs	French	Exp/Very Exp	98	C	2
El Bizcocho	Continental	Expensive	97	C	1
Rancho Valencia Restaurant	California French	Exp/Very Exp	95	B	2
Four-Star Restaurants					
Cafe Pacifica	Seafood	Moderate	94	C	6
Pacifica Del Mar	Seafood/Fusion	Moderate	94	C	2
Prego	Italian	Moderate	94	C	4
Ruth's Chris Steak House	Steaks	Exp/Very Exp	94	D	6
University Club	American	Mod/Exp	94	C	6
Belgian Lion	French	Mod/Exp	93	B	5
Laurel	American	Moderate	93	B	6
Montanas American Grill	American	Inexp/Mod	93	B	6
Panevino	Italian	Moderate	93	D	6
Top o' the Cove	Continental	Expensive	93	C	3
WineSellar and Brasserie	French	Mod/Exp	93	C	4
California Cuisine	California	Moderate	92	B	6
George's at the Cove	California	Mod/Exp	92	C	3
Jasmine	Chinese	Moderate	92	C	4
Piatti	Italian	Moderate	92	C	3
Sally's	Seafood/Mediterranean	Mod/Exp	92	C	6
Bread & Cie	Bakery Cafe	Inexpensive	90	B	6
Chilango's Mexico City Grill	Mexican	Inexpensive	90	A	6
Croce's Restaurant	California	Moderate	90	B	6
Daily's Fit and Fresh	California/Health Food	Inexpensive	90	B	4
Indigo Grill	Southwestern	Inexp/Mod	90	A	6

Name	Cuisine	Price Rating	Quality Rating	Value Rating	Zone
Four-Star Restaurants *(continued)*					
Los Arcos	Mexican/ Seafood	Inexpensive	90	A	8
Prince of Wales Grill	American	Expensive	90	C	8
Rainwater's on Kettner	American	Mod/Exp	90	D	6
Sammy's California Woodfired Pizza	Italian/Pizza	Inexp/Mod	90	B	2,3,6
Souplantation	American	Inexpensive	90	A	1,2,4, 5,7
Trattoria Acqua	Italian	Moderate	90	C	3
Three-Star Restaurants					
Aladdin Mediterranean Cafe	Middle Eastern	Inexpensive	89	B	4
Brendory's by the Sea	Southern/Cajun	Inexpensive	89	B	8
Fins	Mexican	Inexpensive	89	B	1,3,4
Fio's	Italian	Moderate	89	C	6
The Fish Market/ Top of the Market	Seafood	Mod/Exp	89	C	6
Pannikin's Brockton Villa	California	Inexp/Mod	89	B	3
Busalacchi's Ristorante	Italian	Inexp/Mod	88	B	6
Cafe Japengo	Pacific Rim/ Sushi Bar	Inexp/Mod	88	C	4
Cindy Black's	California French	Moderate	88	C	3
Dobson's	California French	Moderate	88	C	6
Emerald Chinese Restaurant	Chinese/Seafood	Inexp/Mod	88	C	4
Islands	American	Inexpensive	88	B	1,4
La Strada	Italian	Moderate	88	C	6
Le Fontainebleau Room	Continental	Expensive	88	C	6
Manhattan	Italian	Mod/Exp	88	C	3
Sorrentino's Ristorante Italiano	Italian	Inexp/Mod	88	B	4

Name	Cuisine	Price Rating	Quality Rating	Value Rating	Zone
Sushi Ota	Japanese / Sushi Bar	Moderate	88	D	5
Thee Bungalow	Continental	Moderate	88	B	5
Zinc Cafe	American	Inexpensive	88	C	2
La Costa	Mexican / Seafood	Moderate	87	B	8
Saffron	Thai / Chicken	Inexpensive	86	A	6
Aesop's Tables	Greek / Mediterranean	Inexp / Mod	85	B	4
Arrivederci Italian Ristorante	Italian	Inexp / Mod	85	D	6
Chez Odette	Deli	Inexpensive	85	B	6
Claim Jumper	American	Inexp / Mod	85	A	1, 2, 7
Epazote	Southwestern	Inexp / Mod	85	C	2
Extraordinary Desserts	Desserts / Coffee	Inexpensive	85	D	6
Grant Grill	Continental	Mod / Exp	85	C	6
Hops! Bistro & Brewery	American	Inexpensive	85	B	4, 6
Rhinoceros Cafe and Grill	American	Inexp / Mod	85	B	8
Shien of Osaka	Japanese	Inexpensive	85	B	1
Vigilucci's Trattoria Italiana	Italian	Inexp / Mod	85	B	2
Bakery Lafayette	Bakery Cafe	Inexpensive	84	B	1
Bernard'O Restaurant	California French	Moderate	84	C	1
Caldo Pomodoro	Italian	Inexp / Mod	84	B	2
Cilantro's	Southwestern	Inexp / Mod	84	C	2
George's Cafe and Ocean Terrace	American	Moderate	84	C	3
Old Town Mexican Cafe	Mexican	Inexpensive	84	B	6
Anthony's Star of the Sea Room	Seafood	Expensive	83	D	6
Trattoria Mannino	Italian	Inexp / Mod	83	B	3
Athens Market Taverna	Greek	Inexp / Mod	82	C	6

Name	Cuisine	Price Rating	Quality Rating	Value Rating	Zone
Three–Star Restaurants *(continued)*					
Banzai Cantina	Japanese / Mexican	Inexp / Mod	82	C	6
El Tecolote	Mexican	Inexpensive	82	B	4
Karinya Thai Cuisine	Thai	Inexpensive	82	C	5
Khyber Pass	Afghani	Inexp / Mod	82	C	4
Monsoon	International / Vegetarian	Inexpensive	82	B	6
Berta's	Latin American	Inexpensive	81	B	6
Cafe Luna	Italian	Inexp / Mod	81	B	1
Oscar's	American	Inexpensive	81	B	1, 2, 4
Salvatore's	Italian	Moderate	81	C	6
Andres' Cuban Restaurant	Cuban	Inexpensive	80	B	4
Bayou Bar & Grill	Creole / Cajun	Moderate	80	C	6
Cafe Champagne	California French	Inexp / Mod	80	C	1
Cafe on Park	American	Inexpensive	80	B	6
D'Lish Gourmet Pasta and Pizza	Italian / Pizza	Inexpensive	80	B	3, 8
D. Z. Aiken's	Deli	Inexpensive	80	B	7
Delicias	California French	Mod / Exp	80	D	2
Emperor's Palace	Chinese	Inexpensive	80	B	1
French Gourmet	California French	Inexp / Mod	80	C	3, 5
Hernandez' Hideaway	Mexican	Inexp / Mod	80	B	1
Ichiban	Japanese	Inexpensive	80	A	5, 6
Karl Strauss' Old Columbia Brewery & Grill	German / American	Inexpensive	80	B	3, 4, 6
Machupicchu	Peruvian	Inexpensive	80	B	5
Milton's	Deli	Inexpensive	80	B	2
Mister A's	Continental	Mod / Exp	80	C	6
Old Town Thai	Thai	Inexpensive	80	B	6
150 Grand Cafe	California	Inexp / Mod	80	C	1
Palenque	Mexican	Inexp / Mod	80	B	5
Panda Inn	Chinese	Inexp / Mod	80	C	6
Pelly's	Seafood	Inexpensive	80	B	2

Name	Cuisine	Price Rating	Quality Rating	Value Rating	Zone
Peohe's	Seafood	Mod/Exp	80	D	8
Pho Pasteur	Vietnamese	Inexpensive	80	B	4
Pizza Nova	Italian/Pizza	Inexpensive	80	C	4,5,6
Sfuzzi	Italian	Inexp/Mod	80	C	6
Thai Chada	Thai	Inexpensive	80	B	5
Wazwan Indian Cuisine	Indian	Inexpensive	80	B	1,4

Two-Star Restaurants

Name	Cuisine	Price Rating	Quality Rating	Value Rating	Zone
A la Francaise	Bakery Cafe	Inexpensive	79	C	6
Carnitas Uruapan	Mexican	Inexpensive	79	B	8
Chino	Southwestern/ Sushi Bar	Mod/Exp	79	D	6
The Corvette Diner, Bar & Grill	American	Inexpensive	79	C	6
Fifth & Hawthorn	California/ Pacific Rim	Moderate	79	C	6
Gelato Vero Caffe	Desserts/Coffee	Inexpensive	79	B	6
Il Fornaio Cucina Italiana/Enoteca Fornaio	Italian	Moderate	79	C	2
Marine Room Restaurant	French	Mod/Exp	79	C	3
Niban Japanese Restaurant	Japanese	Inexpensive	79	A	4
Point Loma Seafoods	Seafood	Inexpensive	79	C	5
Big Stone Lodge	American/ Barbecue	Inexp/Mod	78	C	1
Buffalo Ranch Steakhouse	Steaks/Barbecue	Inexp/Mod	78	B	1
Cafe 222	California	Inexpensive	78	C	6
Cafe Eleven	California French	Inexp/Mod	78	C	6
Cheese Shop	American	Inexpensive	78	C	3,6
French Market Grill	French	Moderate	78	D	1
Solunto Baking Company	Bakery Cafe	Inexpensive	78	B	6
Julian Pie Co.	Desserts	Inexpensive	77	B	1

Name	Cuisine	Price Rating	Quality Rating	Value Rating	Zone
Two-Star Restaurants (*continued*)					
Galaxy Grill	American	Inexpensive	76	B	6
Little Tokyo	Japanese	Inexpensive	76	B	1,6
Sushi Deli	Japanese / Sushi Bar	Inexpensive	76	B	6
Alfonso's	Mexican	Inexp / Mod	75	C	3
Big Kitchen Cafe	American	Inexpensive	75	B	6
Canton Seafood Restaurant	Chinese	Inexpensive	75	B	7
Crest Cafe	American	Inexpensive	75	C	6
Filippi's Pizza Grotto	Italian / Pizza	Inexpensive	75	B	1,6,8
Harry's Cafe Gallery	American	Inexpensive	75	C	3
Jake's Del Mar	American	Moderate	75	C	2,8
Ole Madrid	Spanish / Mediterranean	Moderate	75	D	6
Adam's Steak and Eggs	American / Breakfast	Inexpensive	74	B	4
Rubio's	Mexican	Inexpensive	74	B	1,2,4, 5,6,7
Domenic's Ristorante	Italian	Inexpensive	73	B	1
Le Peep	American	Inexpensive	73	B	1,2
Buffalo Joe's	American / Barbecue	Inexp / Mod	72	C	6
Casa de Bandini	Mexican	Inexp / Mod	72	C	6
El Indio	Mexican	Inexpensive	72	B	5,6
Humphrey's	Seafood	Mod / Exp	72	C	5
Kung Food Vegetarian Restaurant	International / Vegetarian	Inexpensive	72	B	6
Mr. Chow's	Chinese	Inexpensive	72	B	4
Allen's Alley	American	Inexpensive	70	B	1
Anthony's Fish Grotto	Seafood	Inexp / Mod	70	C	1,6,7,8
One-Star Restaurants					
Hob Nob Hill	American	Inexp / Mod	75	B	6
Dick's Last Resort	American	Inexp / Mod	68	C	6
Sportsmen's Seafood	Seafood	Inexpensive	60	D	5

Restaurants by Zone

Name	Star Rating	Price Rating	Quality Rating	Value Rating
Zone 1—North County Inland				
◆ *American*				
Souplantation	★★★★	Inexpensive	90	A
Islands	★★★	Inexpensive	88	B
Claim Jumper	★★★	Inexp/Mod	85	A
Oscar's	★★★	Inexpensive	81	B
Le Peep	★★	Inexpensive	73	B
Allen's Alley	★★	Inexpensive	70	B
◆ *American/Barbecue*				
Big Stone Lodge	★★	Inexp/Mod	78	C
◆ *Bakery Cafe*				
Bakery Lafayette	★★★	Inexpensive	84	B
◆ *California*				
150 Grand Cafe	★★★	Inexp/Mod	80	C
◆ *California French*				
Bernard'O Restaurant	★★★	Moderate	84	C
Cafe Champagne	★★★	Inexp/Mod	80	C
◆ *Chinese*				
Emperor's Palace	★★★	Inexpensive	80	B
◆ *Continental*				
El Bizcocho	★★★★★	Expensive	97	C
◆ *Desserts*				
Julian Pie Co.	★★	Inexpensive	77	B
◆ *French*				
French Market Grill	★★	Moderate	78	D
◆ *Indian*				
Wazwan Indian Cuisine	★★★	Inexpensive	80	B
◆ *Italian*				
Cafe Luna	★★★	Inexp/Mod	81	B
Domenic's Ristorante	★★	Inexpensive	73	B

Name	Star Rating	Price Rating	Quality Rating	Value Rating
◆ *Italian / Pizza*				
Filippi's Pizza Grotto	★★	Inexpensive	75	B
◆ *Japanese*				
Shien of Osaka	★★★	Inexpensive	85	B
Little Tokyo	★★	Inexpensive	76	B
◆ *Mexican*				
Fins	★★★	Inexpensive	89	B
Hernandez' Hideaway	★★★	Inexp / Mod	80	B
Rubio's	★★	Inexpensive	74	B
◆ *Seafood*				
Anthony's Fish Grotto	★★	Inexp / Mod	70	C
◆ *Steaks / Barbecue*				
Buffalo Ranch Steakhouse	★★	Inexp / Mod	78	B
Zone 2—North County Coastal				
◆ *American*				
Souplantation	★★★★	Inexpensive	90	A
Zinc Cafe	★★★	Inexpensive	88	C
Claim Jumper	★★★	Inexp / Mod	85	A
Oscar's	★★★	Inexpensive	81	B
Jake's Del Mar	★★	Moderate	75	C
Le Peep	★★	Inexpensive	73	B
◆ *California French*				
Rancho Valencia Restaurant	★★★★★	Exp / Very Exp	95	B
Delicias	★★★	Mod / Exp	80	D
◆ *Deli*				
Milton's	★★★	Inexpensive	80	B
◆ *French*				
Mille Fleurs	★★★★★	Exp / Very Exp	98	C
◆ *Italian*				
Vigilucci's Trattoria Italiana	★★★	Inexp / Mod	85	B
Caldo Pomodoro	★★★	Inexp / Mod	84	B

Name	Star Rating	Price Rating	Quality Rating	Value Rating
Il Fornaio Cucina Italiana / Enoteca Fornaio	★★	Moderate	79	C
♦ *Italian / Pizza*				
Sammy's California Woodfired Pizza	★★★★	Inexp / Mod	90	B
♦ *Mexican*				
Rubio's	★★	Inexpensive	74	B
♦ *Seafood*				
Pacifica Del Mar	★★★★	Moderate	94	C
The Fish Market / Top of the Market	★★★	Mod / Exp	89	C
Pelly's	★★★	Inexpensive	80	B
♦ *Southwestern*				
Epazote	★★★	Inexp / Mod	85	C
Cilantro's	★★★	Inexp / Mod	84	C
Zone 3—La Jolla				
♦ *American*				
George's Cafe and Ocean Terrace	★★★	Moderate	84	C
Cheese Shop	★★	Inexpensive	78	C
Harry's Cafe Gallery	★★	Inexpensive	75	C
♦ *California*				
George's at the Cove	★★★★	Mod / Exp	92	C
Pannikin's Brockton Villa	★★★	Inexp / Mod	89	B
♦ *California French*				
Cindy Black's	★★★	Moderate	88	C
French Gourmet	★★★	Inexp / Mod	80	C
♦ *Continental*				
Top o' the Cove	★★★★	Expensive	93	C
♦ *French*				
Marine Room Restaurant	★★	Mod / Exp	79	C

Name	Star Rating	Price Rating	Quality Rating	Value Rating
◆ *German / American*				
Karl Strauss' Old Columbia Brewery & Grill	★★★	Inexpensive	80	B
◆ *Italian*				
Piatti	★★★★	Moderate	92	C
Trattoria Acqua	★★★★	Moderate	90	C
Manhattan	★★★	Mod/Exp	88	C
Trattoria Mannino	★★★	Inexp/Mod	83	B
◆ *Italian / Pizza*				
Sammy's California Woodfired Pizza	★★★★	Inexp/Mod	90	B
D'Lish Gourmet Pasta and Pizza	★★★	Inexpensive	80	B
◆ *Mexican*				
Fins	★★★	Inexpensive	89	B
Alfonso's	★★	Inexp/Mod	75	C
Zone 4—Mission Valley and the Mesas				
◆ *Afghani*				
Khyber Pass	★★★	Inexp/Mod	82	C
◆ *American*				
Souplantation	★★★★	Inexpensive	90	A
Islands	★★★	Inexpensive	88	B
Hops! Bistro & Brewery	★★★	Inexpensive	85	B
Oscar's	★★★	Inexpensive	81	B
◆ *American / Breakfast*				
Adam's Steak and Eggs	★★	Inexpensive	74	B
◆ *California*				
Daily's Fit and Fresh	★★★★	Inexpensive	90	B
◆ *Chinese*				
Jasmine	★★★★	Moderate	92	C
Emerald Chinese Restaurant	★★★	Inexp/Mod	88	C
Mr. Chow's	★★	Inexpensive	72	B

Restaurants by Zone (continued)

Name	Star Rating	Price Rating	Quality Rating	Value Rating
◆ *Cuban*				
Andres' Cuban Restaurant	★★★	Inexpensive	80	B
◆ *French*				
WineSellar and Brasserie	★★★★	Mod/Exp	93	C
◆ *German/American*				
Karl Strauss' Old Columbia Brewery & Grill	★★★	Inexpensive	80	B
◆ *Greek/Mediterranean*				
Aesop's Tables	★★★	Inexp/Mod	85	B
◆ *Indian*				
Wazwan Indian Cuisine	★★★	Inexpensive	80	B
◆ *Italian*				
Prego	★★★★	Moderate	94	C
Sorrentino's Ristorante Italiano	★★★	Inexp/Mod	88	B
◆ *Italian/Pizza*				
Pizza Nova	★★★	Inexpensive	80	C
◆ *Japanese*				
Niban Japanese Restaurant	★★	Inexpensive	79	A
◆ *Mexican*				
Fins	★★★	Inexpensive	89	B
El Tecolote	★★★	Inexpensive	82	B
Rubio's	★★	Inexpensive	74	B
◆ *Middle Eastern*				
Aladdin Mediterranean Cafe	★★★	Inexpensive	89	B
◆ *Pacific Rim/Sushi Bar*				
Cafe Japengo	★★★	Inexp/Mod	88	C
◆ *Vietnamese*				
Pho Pasteur	★★★	Inexpensive	80	B

Restaurants by Zone (continued)

Name	Star Rating	Price Rating	Quality Rating	Value Rating
Zone 5—Mission Bay and Beaches				
◆ *American*				
Souplantation	★★★★	Inexpensive	90	A
◆ *California French*				
French Gourmet	★★★	Inexp/Mod	80	C
◆ *Continental*				
Thee Bungalow	★★★	Moderate	88	B
◆ *French*				
Belgian Lion	★★★★	Mod/Exp	93	B
◆ *Italian/Pizza*				
Pizza Nova	★★★	Inexpensive	80	C
◆ *Japanese/Sushi Bar*				
Sushi Ota	★★★	Moderate	88	D
◆ *Mexican*				
Palenque	★★★	Inexp/Mod	80	B
Rubio's	★★	Inexpensive	74	B
El Indio	★★	Inexpensive	72	B
◆ *Peruvian*				
Machupicchu	★★★	Inexpensive	80	B
◆ *Seafood*				
Point Loma Seafoods	★★	Inexpensive	79	C
Humphrey's	★★	Mod/Exp	72	C
Sportsmen's Seafood	★	Inexpensive	60	D
◆ *Thai*				
Karinya Thai Cuisine	★★★	Inexpensive	82	C
Thai Chada	★★★	Inexpensive	80	B
Zone 6—Downtown/Uptown/Central				
◆ *American*				
University Club	★★★★	Mod/Exp	94	C
Laurel	★★★★	Moderate	93	B

Name	Star Rating	Price Rating	Quality Rating	Value Rating
Montanas American Grill	★★★★	Inexp/Mod	93	B
Rainwater's on Kettner	★★★★	Mod/Exp	90	D
Hops! Bistro & Brewery	★★★	Inexpensive	85	B
Cafe on Park	★★★	Inexpensive	80	B
The Corvette Diner, Bar & Grill	★★	Inexpensive	79	C
Cheese Shop	★★	Inexpensive	78	C
Galaxy Grill	★★	Inexpensive	76	B
Big Kitchen Cafe	★★	Inexpensive	75	B
Crest Cafe	★★	Inexpensive	75	C
Hob Nob Hill	★	Inexp/Mod	75	B
Dick's Last Resort	★	Inexp/Mod	68	C

◆ *American / Barbecue*

Buffalo Joe's	★★	Inexp/Mod	72	C

◆ *Bakery Cafe*

Bread & Cie	★★★★	Inexpensive	90	B
A la Francaise	★★	Inexpensive	79	C
Solunto Baking Company	★★	Inexpensive	78	B

◆ *California*

California Cuisine	★★★★	Moderate	92	B
Croce's Restaurant	★★★★	Moderate	90	B
Cafe 222	★★	Inexpensive	78	C

◆ *California French*

Dobson's	★★★	Moderate	88	C
Cafe Eleven	★★	Inexp/Mod	78	C

◆ *California / Pacific Rim*

Fifth & Hawthorn	★★	Moderate	79	C

◆ *Chinese*

Panda Inn	★★★	Inexp/Mod	80	C

◆ *Continental*

Le Fontainebleau Room	★★★	Expensive	88	C
Grant Grill	★★★	Mod/Exp	85	C
Mister A's	★★★	Mod/Exp	80	C

Name	Star Rating	Price Rating	Quality Rating	Value Rating
◆ *Creole / Cajun*				
Bayou Bar & Grill	★★★	Moderate	80	C
◆ *Deli*				
Chez Odette	★★★	Inexpensive	85	B
◆ *Desserts / Coffee*				
Extraordinary Desserts	★★★	Inexpensive	85	D
Gelato Vero Caffe	★★	Inexpensive	79	B
◆ *German / American*				
Karl Strauss' Old Columbia Brewery & Grill	★★★	Inexpensive	80	B
◆ *Greek*				
Athens Market Taverna	★★★	Inexp / Mod	82	C
◆ *International / Vegetarian*				
Monsoon	★★★	Inexpensive	82	B
Kung Food Vegetarian Restaurant	★★	Inexpensive	72	B
◆ *Italian*				
Panevino	★★★★	Moderate	93	D
Fio's	★★★	Moderate	89	C
Busalacchi's Ristorante	★★★	Inexp / Mod	88	B
La Strada	★★★	Moderate	88	C
Arrivederci Italian Ristorante	★★★	Inexp / Mod	85	D
Salvatore's	★★★	Moderate	81	C
Sfuzzi	★★★	Inexp / Mod	80	C
◆ *Italian / Pizza*				
Sammy's California Woodfired Pizza	★★★★	Inexp / Mod	90	B
Pizza Nova	★★★	Inexpensive	80	C
Filippi's Pizza Grotto	★★	Inexpensive	75	B
◆ *Japanese*				
Ichiban	★★★	Inexpensive	80	A
Little Tokyo	★★	Inexpensive	76	B

Name	Star Rating	Price Rating	Quality Rating	Value Rating
◆ *Japanese / Sushi Bar*				
Sushi Deli	★★	Inexpensive	76	B
◆ *Japanese / Mexican*				
Banzai Cantina	★★★	Inexp / Mod	82	C
◆ *Latin American*				
Berta's	★★★	Inexpensive	81	B
◆ *Mexican*				
Chilango's Mexico City Grill	★★★★	Inexpensive	90	A
Old Town Mexican Cafe	★★★	Inexpensive	84	B
Rubio's	★★	Inexpensive	74	B
Casa de Bandini	★★	Inexp / Mod	72	C
El Indio	★★	Inexpensive	72	B
◆ *Seafood*				
Cafe Pacifica	★★★★	Moderate	94	C
The Fish Market / Top of the Market	★★★	Mod / Exp	89	C
Anthony's Star of the Sea Room	★★★	Expensive	83	D
Anthony's Fish Grotto	★★	Inexp / Mod	70	C
◆ *Seafood / Mediterranean*				
Sally's	★★★★	Mod / Exp	92	C
◆ *Southwestern*				
Indigo Grill	★★★★	Inexp / Mod	90	A
◆ *Southwestern / Sushi Bar*				
Chino	★★	Mod / Exp	79	D
◆ *Spanish / Mediterranean*				
Ole Madrid	★★	Moderate	75	D
◆ *Steaks*				
Ruth's Chris Steak House	★★★★	Exp / Very Exp	94	D
Rainwater's on Kettner	★★★★	Mod / Exp	90	D

Name	Star Rating	Price Rating	Quality Rating	Value Rating
◆ Thai				
Saffron	★★★	Inexpensive	86	A
Old Town Thai	★★★	Inexpensive	80	B
Zone 7—San Diego East / East County				
◆ American				
Souplantation	★★★★	Inexpensive	90	A
Claim Jumper	★★★	Inexp / Mod	85	A
◆ Chinese				
Canton Seafood Restaurant	★★	Inexpensive	75	B
◆ Deli				
D. Z. Aiken's	★★★	Inexpensive	80	B
◆ Mexican				
Rubio's	★★	Inexpensive	74	B
◆ Seafood				
Anthony's Fish Grotto	★★	Inexp / Mod	70	C
Zone 8—Coronado / South Bay / Tijuana				
◆ American				
Prince of Wales Grill	★★★★	Expensive	90	C
Rhinoceros Cafe and Grill	★★★	Inexp / Mod	85	B
Jake's Del Mar	★★	Moderate	75	C
◆ California / Mediterranean				
Azzura Point	★★★★★	Expensive	98	B
◆ French				
Marius	★★★★★	Exp / Very Exp	99	B
◆ Italian / Pizza				
D'Lish Gourmet Pasta and Pizza	★★★	Inexpensive	80	B
Filippi's Pizza Grotto	★★	Inexpensive	75	B
◆ Mexican				
Carnitas Uruapan	★★	Inexpensive	79	B
Rubio's	★★	Inexpensive	74	B

Restaurants by Zone (continued)

Name	Star Rating	Price Rating	Quality Rating	Value Rating
◆ *Mexican / Seafood*				
Los Arcos	★★★★	Inexpensive	90	A
La Costa	★★★	Moderate	87	B
◆ *Seafood*				
Peohe's	★★★	Mod / Exp	80	D
Anthony's Fish Grotto	★★	Inexp / Mod	70	C
◆ *Southern / Cajun*				
Brendory's by the Sea	★★★	Inexpensive	89	B

RESTAURANT
profiles

A la Francaise

Bakery Cafe
★★
Inexpensive

Quality 79   Value C

Reservations:	Not accepted
When to go:	Breakfast or lunch
Entree range:	$4–6
Payment:	VISA, MC
Service rating:	★★
Friendliness rating:	★★★
Parking:	Fee lot, street
Bar:	None
Wine selection:	None
Dress:	Informal
Disabled access:	Yes
Customers:	Locals
Breakfast/Lunch:	Monday–Saturday, 7 A.M.–2 P.M.;
	Sunday, 11 A.M.–3 P.M.

Atmosphere/setting: A small local version of a French pâtisserie, boulangerie, and sandwich shop all merged into one. There are a few modest tables where you can sit, drink coffee, and have breakfast or lunch. The setting is pleasant but spare, and geared more to carry-out service.

House specialties: Breads; cakes; quiche Lorraine; croque monsieur; croque madame; chicken crêpes.

Other recommendations: Onion soup; salade Niçoise; mushroom quiche; Provençal omelet; eggs Benedict; banana waffles.

Summary & comments: A la Francaise's specialty is breads and fancy cakes, a modest version of a French pâtisserie and boulangerie. Breads, cakes, tortes, pies, and croissants are baked fresh seven days a week. The few tables provide an opportunity to sit, have pastry and coffee, and try the excellent quiche or any of a half-dozen American-style sandwiches, all served on homemade bread.

Honors & awards: Small Business of the Month, January 1995.

II

Adam's Steak and Eggs

Zone 4   Mission Valley and the Mesas
1201 Hotel Circle South
291-1103

American
★★
Inexpensive
Quality 74   Value B

Reservations:	Not accepted
When to go:	Breakfast
Entree range:	$2–7
Payment:	VISA, MC, AMEX, DC, D
Service rating:	★★
Friendliness rating:	★★
Parking:	Free lot
Bar:	Full service
Wine selection:	House
Dress:	Informal
Disabled access:	No
Customers:	Locals, businesspeople, visitors / tourists
Breakfast:	Monday–Friday, 6:30–11:30 A.M.;
	Saturday and Sunday, 7 A.M.–1 P.M.

Atmosphere / setting: Adam's looks like an Elk's Club in Montana. It's your basic '50s brown wood paneling and formica decor, with nothing new, trendy, or cozy. Just a plain old-fashioned but still robust diner.

House specialties: Steak and eggs; carne asada and eggs; pancakes; waffles; omelets; corn fritters; huevos rancheros.

Other recommendations: Ramos fizz; flapjacks; Denver omelet; sourdough French toast; farmer's omelet.

Entertainment & amenities: Patio dining available.

Summary & comments: As you enter, you'll actually see two restaurants across the lobby from one another. Adam's Steak and Eggs is on the left and is open only in the morning; Albie's Beef Inn is to the right and opens for lunch and dinner. Turn left. Adam's is a thriving local institution that's totally down home, direct, inexpensive, and almost always crowded with a mix of locals who seek it out, as well as tourists who wander in uncertainly. Breakfasts are hearty, waitresses are no-nonsense efficient, and you won't find a fern in the place.

Honors & awards: *San Diego Magazine,* Best Breakfast, Award of Excellence.

52

Aesop's Tables

Zone 4 Mission Valley and the Mesas	Greek/Mediterranean
Costa Verde Shopping Center,	★★★
8650 Genesee Avenue	Inexpensive/Moderate
455-1535	Quality 85 Value B

Reservations:	Only for parties of five or more
When to go:	Dinner
Entree range:	$7–15
Payment:	VISA, MC, AMEX, DC, D
Service rating:	★★
Friendliness rating:	★★★
Parking:	Free lot
Bar:	Full service
Wine selection:	Good
Dress:	Informal
Disabled access:	Yes
Customers:	Locals, visitors/tourists
Lunch:	Monday–Saturday, 11 A.M.–4 P.M.
Dinner:	Sunday and Monday, 4–9 P.M.;
	Tuesday–Saturday, 4–10 P.M.

Atmosphere/setting: Several large rooms, comfortably appointed, and crowded with tables, on the lower level of the Costa Verde shopping center.

House specialties: Gyro plate; leg of lamb; avgolemono soup; saganaki; and bastilla.

Other recommendations: Falafel; char-broiled vegetable salad; sausage pizza; dolmades; grilled salmon in grape leaves; skewer of grilled lamb.

Summary & comments: Aesop's is as much about value as taste. It's a place for solid food, moderate prices, and generous portions. The grilled lamb kebabs are excellent and for under $9 there's a gyro dinner that starts off with egg-lemon soup and moves on to a platter stacked high with thin slices of warm ground lamb surrounded by hunks of onions, tomatoes, and pita. The most exuberantly received dish in the place is the bubbly hot kasseri cheese drizzled with ouzo. When the warm ouzo is ignited at your table and blue flames leap toward the ceiling, everyone in the restaurant seems to yell "Opah!" in unison.

Honors & awards: Best Ethnic/Greek, *San Diego Magazine* Readers' Poll.

Aladdin Mediterranean Cafe

Zone 4   Mission Valley and the Mesas
5420 Clairemont Mesa Boulevard
573-0000

Middle Eastern	
★★★	
Inexpensive	
Quality 89	Value B

Reservations:	Recommended, especially Friday and Saturday nights
When to go:	Any time
Entree range:	$10–12
Payment:	VISA, MC, D
Service rating:	★★
Friendliness rating:	★★★
Parking:	Free lot
Bar:	Limited
Wine selection:	Good
Dress:	Dressy casual, informal
Disabled access:	Yes
Customers:	Locals
Open:	Sunday–Thursday, 11:30 A.M.–9 P.M.; Friday and Saturday, 11:30 A.M.–10 P.M.

Atmosphere / setting: What's odd about the setting is that at your first glance of all the oak trim and smoked glass, it looks like a nice coffee shop or maybe a fast-food restaurant. On closer inspection though, you're aware that all those tables and low partitions are done with awfully expensive materials—but it still looks like a coffee shop.

House specialties: Hummus; falafel; shish kebabs; wood-fired pizza; shawerma of marinated beef and lamb.

Other recommendations: Baba ghanoush; chicken salad with pita bread; vegetarian pizza; chicken sandwich; meze platter; breakfast meze salad.

Summary & comments: Though this is supposed to be a Middle Eastern restaurant—and most foods are indeed from Turkey, Lebanon, and Egypt—there's also representation from Italy, France, and parts of the United States. The very best appetizer is an outstanding garlic and eggplant dip called baba ghanoush, though equally wonderful are the thin, shaved slices of rotisseried beef and lamb served inside a pita with a creamy garlic sauce. One of the biggest surprises is a sensational vegetarian pizza. There's also a terrific grilled-chicken salad that's both enormous and tasty. All this good food in such a modest setting remains a bit startling regardless of how many times you visit.

Alfonso's

Zone 3   La Jolla
1251 Prospect Street
454-2232

	Mexican
	★★
	Inexpensive/Moderate
	Quality 75 Value C

Reservations:	Only for six or more
When to go:	Any time on a beautiful day
Entree range:	$7–16
Payment:	VISA, MC, AMEX
Service rating:	★★
Friendliness rating:	★★★
Parking:	Valet, street
Bar:	Full service
Wine selection:	Good
Dress:	Dressy casual, informal
Disabled access:	No
Customers:	Locals
Open:	Every day, 11 A.M.–2 A.M.

Atmosphere/setting: Indoor and outdoor seating areas, comfortable and casual Mexicana.

House specialties: Strawberry margaritas; nachos, regular or with carne asada, shredded chicken, or Mexican sausage; fajitas de pollo or carne; diced ham quesadilla.

Other recommendations: Tostada supreme; shrimp burrito; shrimp soup; steak or chicken on a stick; cheese enchiladas.

Summary & comments: The thing about Alfonso's is not so much the food, which is good enough, but the environment. Clientele sometimes get overly happy (though rarely rambunctious), but young and old alike recognize that there are few opportunities to sit outdoors along Prospect Street—which is La Jolla's equivalent of the Grand Canal—and sip margaritas and munch on nachos. It's a grand pastime, especially on balmy evenings and weekends, and that's when there's always a crush to get in.

Allen's Alley

Zone 1   North County Inland
124 Hanes Place, Vista
726-4433

	American
	★ ★
	Inexpensive
	Quality 70 Value B

Reservations:	Not accepted
When to go:	Breakfast
Entree range:	$3–6
Payment:	Cash only
Service rating:	★ ★ ★
Friendliness rating:	★ ★ ★
Parking:	Free lot, street
Bar:	None
Wine selection:	None
Dress:	Informal
Disabled access:	Yes
Customers:	Locals
Breakfast/Lunch:	Monday–Friday, 6 A.M.–3 P.M.;
	Saturday, 7 A.M.–2 P.M.; Sunday, 7 A.M.–1 P.M.

Atmosphere/setting: It's a diner less than half the size of a dining car. There are six formica wood-grained tables and an L-shaped counter with ten moveable caneback chairs. An old Frigidaire sits behind the counter with photos of kids stuck on with magnets.

House specialties: Various omelets; corned beef hash; pork chops and eggs; biscuits and gravy. At lunchtime there's turkey with dressing, BLTs, and patty melts.

Summary & comments: It's a little tricky finding this freestanding cinder-block building since Hanes Place is a one way street—originally an alley. You can only enter off East Vista Street, which is a main thoroughfare. New owners have brightened up the place considerably but they can't alter the basic nature of Allen's Alley, which is a remnant of long-gone '40s America. Local businesspeople wander in and are greeted by name, and they sit down to big breakfasts with eggs and home fries and typically pour on ketchup and several dollops from the bottle of hot sauce that's on every table. Except for breakfast very little of the food is homemade, and that's probably why mornings are the busiest at Allen's Alley. Its authenticity makes it a terrific place to take foreign visitors and introduce them to biscuits and gravy.

Andrés' Cuban Restaurant

	Cuban
	★★★
Zone 4 Mission Valley and the Mesas	Inexpensive
1235 Morena Boulevard	
275-4114	Quality 80 Value B

Reservations:	Accepted
When to go:	Any time
Entree range:	Lunch $4–8, dinner $7–14
Payment:	VISA, MC, AMEX, DC
Service rating:	★★
Friendliness rating:	★★★
Parking:	Street
Bar:	Limited
Wine selection:	House
Dress:	Informal
Disabled access:	Yes
Customers:	Visitors/tourists, ethnic
Lunch:	Tuesday–Saturday, 11 A.M.–4 P.M.; Sunday and Monday, closed.
Dinner:	Tuesday–Saturday, 5–9 P.M.; Sunday and Monday, closed.

Atmosphere/setting: It's all a bit funky. The original seating area is a narrow concrete patio that was once open, but has been roofed over. There's a newer, larger dining room that feels like a mobile home that's about to move—although this mobile home has been fit with greenhouse windows.

House specialties: Black bean soup; empanadas; arroz con pollo; Cuban sandwiches; roast pork with yuca and garlic sauce; paella (served Wednesday night only, or with 24-hour advance notice).

Other recommendations: Fish sautéed with olives and garlic; top sirloin with onions, parsley, and lemon wedges; shredded beef simmered with onions; squid with black rice.

Summary & comments: A family-run business that started out as a roofed-over space between two buildings, Andrés' has expanded over the years but still radiates a sense of impermanence. At lunch you order at a counter and food is brought to you; at dinner there's table service. Most food is surprisingly mild, so if you want additional heat, you have to ask. Several dishes (typically sandwiches at lunch and chicken at night) are cooked under a weight, so they arrive cartoonishly flat and compressed, like a ton of bricks fell on them. A Latin American market used to be at the back of the restaurant but it has expanded and moved to a space almost next door.

Anthony's Fish Grotto

	Seafood
	★★
	Inexpensive / Moderate
	Quality 70 Value C

Zone 1   North County Inland
11666 Avena Place
451-1788

Zone 6   Downtown / Uptown / Central
1360 North Harbor Drive
232-5103

Zone 7   San Diego East / East County
9530 Lake Murray Drive, La Mesa
463-0368

Zone 8   Coronado / South Bay / Tijuana
215 Bay Boulevard, Chula Vista
425-4200

Reservations:	Not accepted
When to go:	Any time
Entree range:	$7–14
Payment:	VISA, MC, AMEX, DC, D
Service rating:	★★
Friendliness rating:	★★
Parking:	Street
Bar:	Full service
Wine selection:	Good
Dress:	Informal
Disabled access:	Yes
Customers:	Locals, visitors / tourists
Open:	Every day, 11:30 A.M.–8:30 P.M.

Atmosphere / setting: The Harbor Drive restaurant is very much like a lunchroom right on the waterfront. It's bright, efficient, spacious, and cafeteria-like.

House specialties: Coconut fried shrimp; fish and chips; broiled red snapper; halibut; swordfish; combination seafood salads; simply prepared items.

Other recommendations: Clam tenders; calamari cutlets; cioppino casserole; linguine with shrimp; broiled lobster.

Summary & comments: There are a number of Anthony's in the San Diego area, and they're all still run by the same local family. In character, they range from the very informal (as on North Harbor Drive) to more of a dinnerhouse decor. They are frequented mostly by tourists who are attracted by the setting and by an older local crowd that likes the predictability.

Honors & awards: Readers' Award, *San Diego Union;* Best Seafood, *San Diego Magazine;* Best Seafood, San Diego Restaurant Association.

Anthony's Star of the Sea Room

	Seafood
	★★★
	Expensive
Zone 6 Mission Valley and the Mesas	
1360 North Harbor Drive	Quality 83 Value D
232-7408	

Reservations:	Recommended
When to go:	Any time
Entree range:	$18–32
Payment:	VISA, MC, AMEX, DC, D
Service rating:	★★★
Friendliness rating:	★★★★
Parking:	Street, valet
Bar:	Full service
Wine selection:	Extensive
Dress:	Dressy, dressy casual; men are required to wear jackets
Disabled access:	Yes
Customers:	Locals, visitors/tourists
Dinner:	Every day, 5:30–10:30 P.M.

Atmosphere/setting: There's a time warp–look to the room that takes you back to the 1970s. There are formal chandeliers and smoked-glass panels, and both the walls and arches are covered in wood shingles, so it looks like the setting was once more informal. Two walls are nothing but glass windows facing San Diego Bay. It's a stunning view, especially at night.

House specialties: Fresh fish and seafood: abalone, salmon, scallops, halibut, Maine lobster, crab, clams, mussels.

Summary & comments: The Star of the Sea Room is a formal restaurant stuck in the past. Older people (60-plus) who've lived in San Diego a long time tend to love it; younger people tend to dismiss it. The variety of seafood available is impressive, and many dishes are prepared in classic ways that typically involve butter and cream. There's so much flambéeing and tableside service going on, it's miraculous that the place hasn't gone up in smoke.

ARRivEdERci ItaliaN RistoraNTE

<table>
<tr><td></td><td>Italian
★★★</td></tr>
</table>

ARRivEdERci ItaliaN RistoraNTE	Italian ★★★
Zone 6 Downtown/Uptown/Central 3845 Fourth Avenue 299-6282	Inexpensive/Moderate Quality 85 Value D

Reservations:	Recommended
When to go:	Any time
Entree range:	$7–15
Payment:	VISA, MC, AMEX, D
Service rating:	★★★
Friendliness rating:	★★★
Parking:	Fee lot, street
Bar:	None
Wine selection:	Good
Dress:	Dressy casual, informal
Disabled access:	Yes
Customers:	Locals, business
Lunch:	Every day, 11:30 A.M.–2:30 P.M.
Dinner:	Sunday–Thursday, 5–10:30 P.M.; Friday and Saturday, 5–11 P.M.

Atmosphere/setting: Casual, charming, and mildly romantic, with wood trim and pale stucco walls, it's the very image of a neighborly Italian restaurant. When the temperature's cool outside, all dining is inside; but when the weather cooperates, an entire wall of doors opens to the street and inside and outside merge.

House specialties: Grilled vegetables; veal cutlet with tomato and arugula; angelhair pasta with julienned chicken; linguine with clams, mussels, and shrimp; shrimp with garlic and white wine.

Other recommendations: Vegetable omelet; warm spinach salad with smoked duck, pine nuts, and raisins; gnocchi with a cream sauce; pasta and garbanzo bean soup; veal scaloppine with lemon.

Summary & comments: Located in a San Diego neighborhood where hip, gay, and straight converge, Arrivederci is sited on one of the quieter side streets— so if you sit outdoors, you're not overcome by noise and carbon monoxide. There's less street scene to watch, and the pleasure of the day is its own reward. Inside, the walls are filled with photos that look like they're from an old family album, including slightly blurred street scenes and group shots in a dusty Italian hill town, probably taken just after the turn of the century. The sense of nostalgia is palpable, and it casts a soft spell over the entire room. The food is good, but the setting makes it better.

Athens Market Taverna

Zone 6 Downtown/Uptown/Central	Greek
109 West F Street	★★★
234-1955	Inexpensive/Moderate
	Quality 82 Value C

Reservations:	Recommended
When to go:	Any time, but especially Saturday night
Entree range:	Lunch, $5–13; dinner, $10–22
Payment:	VISA, MC, AMEX, DC, D, others
Service rating:	★★★
Friendliness rating:	★★★★
Parking:	Street
Bar:	Full service
Wine selection:	Extensive
Dress:	Dressy casual, informal
Disabled access:	Yes
Customers:	Locals, businesspeople, visitors/tourists
Breakfast:	Monday–Saturday, 7:30–11 A.M.; Sunday, closed.
Lunch:	Monday–Saturday, 11:30 A.M.–4 P.M.; Sunday, closed.
Dinner:	Every day, 4–11 P.M.

Atmosphere/setting: It's nicer and more formal than most Greek restaurants. The breakfast room actually has a gilded turn-of-the-century look. But most of the action is in the main dining room which is wide and shallow, dominated by a handsome bar. A larger dining room is used mostly on weekends.

House specialties: Taramasalata; saganaki; lentil soup; avgolemono soup; lakaniko sausage; lamb chops; lemon chicken; moussaka.

Other recommendations: Vegetarian moussaka; spanakopita; gyro plate; roast leg of lamb; Greek combination plates.

Entertainment & amenities: Belly dancing on Friday and Saturday nights. Teenage boys enter puberty rapidly after a belly dancer ropes them with a silk scarf.

Summary & comments: There are more sparks here than at your average electrical substation, and only half of it comes from the food. Take it for granted that the melted kefalograviera cheese appetizer flaming with brandy is terrific and the spanakopita is darn good. At lunch, the sausage flecked with orange rind and cloaked in pita is immensely satisfying. It all works wonderfully only because Mary Papas, owner/greeter/diva and overseer of it all, not only seems to be everywhere, she is. Her energy fills the room.

Honors & awards: San Diego Restaurant Association, Gold Medallion; Southern California Restaurant Writers, Best Greek.

AZZURA POINT

	California / Mediterranean
Zone 8 Coronado /	★★★★★
South Bay / Tijuana	Expensive
Loews Coronado Bay Resort,	
4000 Coronado Bay Road, Coronado	Quality 98 Value B
424-4000	

Reservations:	Highly recommended
When to go:	Dinner
Entree range:	$17–22
Payment:	VISA, MC, AMEX, DC
Service rating:	★★★★
Friendliness rating:	★★★★
Parking:	Free lot with validation; valet
Bar:	Full service
Wine selection:	Good
Dress:	Dressy casual
Disabled access:	Yes
Customers:	Locals, visitors / tourists
Dinner:	Sunday–Thursday, 6–10 P.M.;
	Friday and Saturday, 6–11 P.M.

Atmosphere / setting: Casually elegant, with a whitewashed finish on tables, chairs, and floors. Waterfront views.

House specialties: Maple-roasted ostrich; abalone ravioli; lobster and goat cheese chile relleno; pepper-crusted ahi; sea bass in potato crust; whole crispy catfish; grilled veal T-bone; herb-crusted rack of lamb.

Other recommendations: Chinese-style smoked lobster; grilled salmon; spit-roasted chicken; swordfish wrapped in bacon; skate salad.

Summary & comments: The nautical character of this seemingly breezy and informal restaurant belies its devotion to high drama and Pacific Rim flavors. Every presentation—every plate delivered—yields a sense of astonishment and a chorus of "wows." Chinese-style smoked lobster and a whole crispy catfish are feasts of both visual splendor and extraordinary taste. It's a place for great food, strong character, and theatrical delivery—which means it is not for the strictly conventional or faint of heart. It is an L.A. sort of place, with more character than a Dickens novel and enough flair for a Danielle Steele potboiler. It leaves diners both breathless and satisfied.

Bakery Lafayette

Bakery Cafe
★★★
Inexpensive

Quality 84   Value B

Zone 1   North County Inland
11828 Rancho Bernardo Road #105
487-0418

Reservations:	Accepted
When to go:	Any time
Entree range:	$4–6
Payment:	Cash, checks
Service rating:	★★
Friendliness rating:	★★★
Parking:	Free lot
Bar:	None
Wine selection:	None
Dress:	Informal
Disabled access:	Yes
Customers:	Locals, businesspeople
Open:	Every day, 7 A.M.–7 P.M.

Atmosphere / setting: Tile floors, glass showcases filled with pastries, and a sense of controlled frenzy. There are three or four tables inside and another half-dozen outside. It's mostly atmosphere-less except for the French accents belonging to the folks behind the counter.

House specialties: Fish dishes; pâté; specialty cakes; baguettes; olive bread; country bread; croissants; breakfast pastries; rugalach; handmade chocolates.

Other recommendations: Salads; quiches; sandwiches; biscotti.

Summary & comments: There's a small breakfast and lunch menu available at this tiny bakery, though it's supplemented by three or four daily specials. Operated by expatriates from Marius—one of the best dining rooms in town—Bakery Lafayette resembles a mom-and-pop operation rather than a venue of some very sophisticated bakers. That's part of its charm though, and it helps makes the place comfortable and homey. After breakfast, lunch, or dinner, many folks buy one or more loaves of bread—and start eating them before leaving the bakery.

Honors & awards: The Best Bakery in America.

Banzai Cantina

Zone 6   Downtown/Uptown/Central
3667 India Street
298-6388

Japanese/Mexican	
★★★	
Inexpensive/Moderate	
Quality 82 Value C	

Reservations: Accepted
When to go: Dinner
Entree range: Lunch, $6–9; dinner, $12–17
Payment: VISA, MC, AMEX, DC, D
Service rating: ★★★
Friendliness rating: ★★★★
Parking: Free lot, street
Bar: Full service
Wine selection: Good
Dress: Dressy casual, informal
Disabled access: Yes
Customers: Locals, businesspeople
Lunch: Every day, 11 A.M.–5 P.M.
Dinner: Sunday and Monday, 5–9 P.M.; Tuesday–Thursday,
                         5–10 P.M.; Friday and Saturday, 5–11 P.M.

Atmosphere/setting: A drop-in neighborhood restaurant, nicely and informally done, with a cordial and chatty staff. There's a small bar and an upstairs dining room that tends to be quieter than the downstairs one.

House specialties: Traditional Japanese and Mexican fare, with some crossover Pacific Rim dishes. Sushi; sashimi; tempura; angelhair pasta with shrimp and black beans; sea bass steamed with miso and cilantro.

Other recommendations: Among the Japanese: sashimi, yakitori, and tempura. Among the Mexican: tomatillo soup, enchiladas, flautas, chicken quesadillas, and carne asada. Among the hybrids: Japanese bouillabaisse, Japanese paella, and ahi with a teriyaki cream sauce.

Summary & comments: This is an informal local eatery that's sufficiently idiosyncratic (and witty) to offer food from Japan and Mexico and beer from everywhere. It probably doesn't hurt that the owner/chef really is named José Kelley. The cross-cultural items—the ones that ignore all national boundaries— are among the best. As well, the Banzai will accommodate special requests and prepare any menu to suit dietary restrictions.

Bayou Bar & Grill

Zone 6   Downtown/Uptown/Central
329 Market Street
696-8747

Creole/Cajun
★★★
Moderate

Quality 80   Value C

Reservations:	Recommended
When to go:	Any time, but especially weekend evenings
Entree range:	$12–17
Payment:	VISA, MC, AMEX, DC, D
Service rating:	★★
Friendliness rating:	★★★
Parking:	Street
Bar:	Full service
Wine selection:	Extensive
Dress:	Dressy casual
Disabled access:	Yes
Customers:	Locals, businesspeople, visitors/tourists
Brunch:	Sunday, 11:30 A.M.–3 P.M.
Lunch:	Wednesday–Sunday, 11:30 A.M.–3 P.M.
Dinner:	Sunday–Thursday, 5–10 P.M.;
	Friday and Saturday, 5–11 P.M.

Atmosphere/setting: Bright, unpretentious, and busy, with tile floors, high ceilings, and windows all across the front of the restaurant, the Bayou feels as much like a modern chop house as a Cajun diner. New Orleans memorabilia is scattered about.

House specialties: Jambalaya; stuffed smoked pork chops; crawfish étouffée; soft-shell crabs; panéed alligator.

Other recommendations: Crawfish omelet; filet mignon royale; Creole cordon bleu; eggplant lagniappe; blackened catfish.

Summary & comments: Cajun and Creole cookery doesn't have much of a foothold in San Diego, so the Bayou is one of about three places offering traditional Louisiana cooking. Most of the dining is indoors, but there's a small outdoor eating area. Fresh seafood is flown in from the Gulf Coast and the Bayou region, and fresh crawfish are almost always available. There are occasionally fixed-price dinner specials when four-course meals are available for around $13, but they're typically offered only one night a week. The Bayou has been experimenting with operating hours, so be sure to call first to make certain they're open for lunch.

Honors & awards: Channel 8 Best Meal 1990; San Diego Resturant Association Best Ethnic Dining 1992; *Travel Holiday* magazine Good Value Dining Award 1992.

Belgian Lion

<table>
<tr><td></td><td>French</td></tr>
<tr><td>Zone 5   Mission Bay and Beaches</td><td>★★★★</td></tr>
<tr><td>2265 Bacon Street</td><td>Moderate / Expensive</td></tr>
<tr><td>223-2700</td><td>Quality 93   Value B</td></tr>
</table>

Reservations:	Highly recommended
When to go:	Dinner
Entree range:	$16.50–21.50
Payment:	VISA, MC, AMEX, DC, D
Service rating:	★★
Friendliness rating:	★★★★
Parking:	Free lot
Bar:	None
Wine selection:	Extensive
Dress:	Dressy casual
Disabled access:	Yes
Customers:	Locals, visitors / tourists
Dinner:	Thursday–Saturday, 5–10 P.M.

Atmosphere / setting: Old World and English manor house flavor; also a bit worn, like an heirloom rug that's been used for a few generations.

House specialties: Salmon with sorrel sauce; cassoulet; confit of duck.

Other recommendations: Marinated herring with crème fraîche; asparagus with strawberry vinaigrette; onion soup; seared sea scallops; rabbit in red wine; choucroute alsacienne.

Summary & comments: Very much a family operation; the husband and wife are owner / chefs, their adult children host and serve, and grandchildren serve and clear. Though the setting is formal, the aura of faded gentility is strong. All dinners come with a variety of well-cooked seasonal vegetables, and the more folks in your party, the more side dishes you'll receive. On a first visit at least one person in any group should order the cassoulet since some of it has been on the stove for the full two decades that the Belgian Lion has been in operation—and it's still sensational.

Bernard'O Restaurant

California French
★★★
Moderate

Quality 84   Value C

Zone 1   North County Inland
12457 Rancho Bernardo Road
487-7171

Reservations:	Recommended
When to go:	Any time
Entree range:	$11–19
Payment:	VISA, MC, AMEX, DC, D
Service rating:	★★
Friendliness rating:	★★
Parking:	Free lot
Bar:	Full service
Wine selection:	Extensive
Dress:	Dressy casual
Disabled access:	Yes
Customers:	Locals, visitors / tourists
Lunch:	Tuesday–Friday, 11:30 A.M.–2 P.M.; Saturday–Monday, closed.
Dinner:	Tuesday–Sunday, 5:30–9 P.M.; Monday, closed.

Atmosphere / setting: With soft lighting, banquettes, and pastoral paintings, it's as country French as you can get in a small suburban shopping center next to a barber shop and a recently abandoned hardware store. Indoor and outdoor seating is available.

House specialties: Snails with white wine; French onion soup; spinach salad with potato pancakes; duck confit with Madeira sauce; filet mignon with caramelized shallots.

Other recommendations: Grilled scallops with lemon and garlic; grilled chicken breast with artichoke bottoms; braised salmon with leeks.

Entertainment & amenities: Live music on holidays.

Summary & comments: As ex-maître d' of the very formal fine dining room at the nearby Rancho Bernardo Inn, Bernard Mougel has created a mini–fine dining experience in his own restaurant. Mougel is always present and watches over the room like a proud and anxious parent concerned that everything works out properly. And notwithstanding the Bernard'O belief in traditional French preparations, the magic of the Mediterranean diet has obviously been a help to M. Mougel: he's run the Boston Marathon a few times.

Honors & awards: *San Diego Magazine* Readers' Poll Best of the Best and Best Service 1994; *Rancho Magazine* Dining Survey Best Gourmet Cuisine 1994–1995.

BERTA'S

Zone 6   Downtown/Uptown/Central
3928 Twiggs Street
295-2343

Latin American
★ ★ ★
Inexpensive
Quality 81   Value B

Reservations:	Recommended for dinner
When to go:	Dinner
Entree range:	$8–13
Payment:	VISA, MC, AMEX
Service rating:	★ ★
Friendliness rating:	★ ★ ★
Parking:	Free lot, street
Bar:	Beer and wine only
Wine selection:	Limited
Dress:	Informal
Disabled access:	Yes
Customers:	Locals, visitors/tourists
Open:	Every day, 11 A.M.–10 P.M.

Atmosphere/setting: Though it's in a freestanding block building, Berta's looks like a creaky old house. The simple interior decor—brown booths and tables covered with white cloths and clear plastic—is meant to be formal but turns out quirky and casual instead, like an aging hacienda. Outdoor tables as well.

House specialties: Paella; Costa Rican casado (black beans, rice, and sautéed plantains); Guatemalan pork casserole; grilled chicken in a smoked jalapeño sauce; Colombian banana leaf tamale; flank steak marinated in lime.

Other recommendations: Beef Trinidad; grilled chicken breast with a spicy chile, almond, and chocolate mole sauce; pasta with a Brazilian peanut and coconut sauce; red potatoes with feta cheese; plantain stuffed with black beans; sautéed masa harina with cheese, topped with sour cream and red salsa.

Summary & comments: There are no more than a dozen tables inside, so the outdoor tables almost double the capacity of Berta's. If you go at lunchtime, you'll wonder how they stay in business; if you go at night, the place is so mobbed you'll be lucky to get in. That's when reservations are essential. The menu intends to cover all of Central and South America, and it handles that immense geography through nomenclature: virtually every dish bears the name of a Latin American country. There are a number of vegetarian dishes on the menu and all the chickens used are hormone-free.

Big Kitchen Cafe

	American
Zone 6 Downtown/Uptown/Central	★★
3003 Grape Street	Inexpensive
234-5789	
	Quality 75 Value B

Reservations:	Only for parties of 6 or more
When to go:	Breakfast
Entree range:	$2–8
Payment:	Cash only
Service rating:	★★
Friendliness rating:	★★★★
Parking:	Street
Bar:	None
Wine selection:	None
Dress:	Very informal
Disabled access:	No
Customers:	Locals
Breakfast/Lunch:	Monday–Friday, 7 A.M.–2 P.M.;
	Saturday and Sunday, 7 A.M.–3 P.M.

Atmosphere/setting: The neighborhood is what you'd call "transitional" and the decor is chockablock mementos and clippings. The lunch counter is the focus of the restaurant—it used to be the entire restaurant—but expansion has allowed for an increase in tables in the main and adjacent rooms. It's the ultimate in casual.

House specialties: Waffles; pancakes; omelets; homemade cakes and muffins; tofu rancheros; spinach lasagna; roast turkey dinners.

Other recommendations: Chorizo and eggs; French toast; baked ham sandwich; black bean chili; falafel.

Summary & comments: The political heart and emotional soul of the neighborhood it operates in, the Big Kitchen is known as much for community activism and its tireless always-stomping-for-a-cause-owner (Judy the Beauty Forman) as it is for hearty down-home breakfasts. Whoopie Goldberg washed dishes here when she was perfecting her stand-up act and returns occasionally to help with one of Forman's frequent benefits and fundraisers. There are also periodic dinner theater productions. If you've ever hankered to explore existentialism over chorizo and eggs, this is the place.

Big Stone Lodge

	Barbecue	
	★★	
	Inexpensive / Moderate	
	Quality 78	Value C

Zone 1   North County Inland
12237 Old Pomerado Road, Poway
748-1617

Reservations:	Recommended
When to go:	Dinner
Entree range:	$6–12
Payment:	VISA, MC, AMEX, D
Service rating:	★★
Friendliness rating:	★★
Parking:	Free lot
Bar:	Full service
Wine selection:	Good
Dress:	Informal
Disabled access:	Yes
Customers:	Locals, visitors / tourists
Brunch:	Sunday, 10:30 A.M.–2 P.M.
Lunch:	Tuesday–Friday, 11:30 A.M.–1:30 P.M.; Saturday–Monday, closed.
Dinner:	Tuesday–Saturday, 5–9 P.M.; Sunday, 2:30–7:30 P.M.; Monday, closed.

Atmosphere / setting: There are two rooms and a bar, and all of it is simple, rustic, and woody. Much of the building was constructed in the late 1920s using boulders from the surrounding hills. There's a large wooden dance floor in the room with the bar.

House specialties: Santa Maria–style barbecue, which involves cooking seasoned meats and poultry over red oak coals.

Other recommendations: Rib-eye steak; pork and beef ribs; Portuguese sausage; barbecued chicken sandwich; grilled salmon.

Entertainment & amenities: Live country music Fridays and Saturdays at 9 P.M.

Summary & comments: Though it's had a couple of names and not always a sociable reputation in its long career, the Big Stone Lodge has consistently been a place where the Old West seems lively and well. There's a lot of line dancing that goes on (instructions are given several nights a week), and many of the patrons come in their cleanest jeans and cowboy boots, drink beer from longneck bottles, and order the unusual Santa Maria–style barbecue that's become the hallmark of the Lodge.

70

Bread & Cie

Zone 6   Downtown/Uptown/Central
350 University Avenue
683-9322

Bakery Cafe	
★★★★	
Inexpensive	
Quality 90	Value B

Reservations:	Not accepted
When to go:	Breakfast or lunch
Entree range:	$2–5
Payment:	Cash or check
Service rating:	★★★
Friendliness rating:	★★★★
Parking:	Free lot, street
Bar:	None
Wine selection:	None
Dress:	Informal
Disabled access:	Yes
Customers:	Locals
Open:	Monday–Friday, 7 A.M.–7 P.M.;
	Saturday, 8 A.M.–6 P.M.; Sunday, 8 A.M.–2 P.M.

Atmosphere/setting: It not only looks like a warehouse with a few tables for very casual eating, that's exactly what it is.

House specialties: Cream cheese and mascarpone with toasted walnuts and cucumbers on fig/anise bread; Black Forest ham with papaya salsa on rye; roast turkey with hot pepper cheese on rosemary bread; rosemary shortbread; classic French tuna salad sandwich.

Other recommendations: Old World hearth-baked country breads; ginger/pear scones.

Summary & comments: The brainchild of a young couple fleeing the accelerated tempo of Los Angeles, Bread & Cie is a working commercial bakery that's added a few tables at which they serve a modest breakfast and lunch featuring Bread & Cie baked goods. All the breads use natural starters, and all are shaped by hand and get several risings. Chats with the owners or the baker happen easily and convivially in an enlarged and modern version of the neighborhood bakery. Many of the breads served in local restaurants come from here. They'll do any of their sandwiches on breads of your choice. Some of the best breads are anise/fig and jalapeño/cheese, though curious ones like chocolate sour cherry challah keep popping up and insisting you taste them. The rosemary shortbread is delicious.

Brendory's by the Sea

Zone 8 Coronado / South Bay / Tijuana	Southern / Cajun
	★★★
Silver Strand Shopping Center, 600 Palm Avenue, Imperial Beach	Inexpensive
423-3991	Quality 89 Value B

Reservations:	Accepted
When to go:	Any time
Entree range:	$5–16
Payment:	VISA, MC, DC, D
Service rating:	★
Friendliness rating:	★★★
Parking:	Free lot, street
Bar:	None
Wine selection:	Limited
Dress:	Informal
Disabled access:	Yes
Customers:	Locals, visitors / tourists
Lunch:	Every day, 11 A.M.–3 P.M.
Dinner:	Monday–Thursday, 3–9 P.M.;
	Friday and Saturday, 3–10 P.M.;
	Sunday, 11 A.M.–7 P.M.

Atmosphere / setting: After three moves into increasingly less formal settings, Brendory's has now landed in a once-Mexican restaurant where you order at a counter and food is delivered when it's ready. Most items are available in small or large plates, and priced accordingly.

House specialties: Red beans and rice with andouille sausage; gumbo; jambalaya; fried catfish; smothered pork chops; walnut sweet potato pie; brandied peach cobbler.

Other recommendations: Boiled shrimp dinner; liver and onion sandwich; catfish Creole; fried clam strips; alligator étouffée.

Summary & comments: One of San Diegans' few options for southern / soul / Louisiana cooking, Brendory's is a family-run operation specializing in large portions of very home-style cooking. The setting is amiable and the food is predictably good. It's not fancy, mind you, just very good. And after your entree, even if you can't manage another bite of food, order a slice of sweet potato pie for the table so you can assure yourself a terrific gilding-the-lily ending.

Buffalo Joe's

	Barbecue
	★★
	Inexpensive / Moderate
	Quality 72 Value C

Zone 6   Downtown / Uptown / Central
600 Fifth Avenue
236-1616

Reservations:	Accepted
When to go:	Any time, but especially on weekends
Entree range:	$6–19
Payment:	VISA, MC, AMEX, DC, D
Service rating:	★★
Friendliness rating:	★★★
Parking:	Street, valet on Fridays and Saturdays
Bar:	Full service
Wine selection:	Good
Dress:	Informal
Disabled access:	Yes
Customers:	Locals, visitors / tourists
Lunch:	Every day, 11 A.M.–3 P.M.
Dinner:	Every day, 3–10 P.M.

Atmosphere / setting: Raw wood and ersatz country western, like the union of *Bonanza* and *HeeHaw.*

House specialties: Barbecued beef, pork, and baby-back ribs; alligator; buffalo burger; stew and chili; buffalo wings; barbecued shrimp.

Other recommendations: Things that get smoked, barbecued, or fried. Chicken; catfish; collard greens; potato salad; onion rings; chili.

Summary & comments: A novelty restaurant where the tasty and the tasteless happily comingle. Food is more aptly considered grub and service sometimes borders on the comic, but enough of the items are savory to warrant a visit or two. Take the kids for lunch or an early dinner and no one will even notice if they throw a tantrum or two.

Honors & awards: *Union Tribune* Reader's Guide Best BBQ; *San Diego Magazine* Best BBQ in San Diego; Unknown Eater, Channel 8, Best Meal.

Buffalo Ranch Steakhouse

<table>
<tr><td>Steaks</td></tr>
<tr><td>★★</td></tr>
<tr><td>Inexpensive/Moderate</td></tr>
<tr><td>Quality 78   Value B</td></tr>
</table>

Zone 1   North County Inland
775 Center Drive, San Marcos
747-9111

Reservations:	Recommended
When to go:	Any time
Entree range:	$13–18
Payment:	VISA, MC, AMEX, D
Service rating:	★★
Friendliness rating:	★★★
Parking:	Free lot
Bar:	Full service
Wine selection:	Good
Dress:	Informal
Disabled access:	Yes
Customers:	Locals, visitors/tourists
Lunch:	Monday–Friday, 11 A.M.–4 P.M.;
	Saturday and Sunday, noon–4 P.M.
Dinner:	Monday–Thursday, 4–10 P.M.;
	Friday and Saturday, 4–11 P.M.; Sunday, 4–9 P.M.

Atmosphere/setting: It looks like a Western ranch house that Ralph Lauren might have selected for a photo shoot. There's a big stone fireplace, lots of wooden booths, and a buffalo head over the bar that occasionally snorts smoke through its nostrils.

House specialties: Hickory-smoked prime rib; chicken; ribs; steaks.

Other recommendations: Buffalo wing sandwich; honey-glazed chicken; New York strip steak; smoked chicken fettuccine; Idaho trout.

Summary & comments: Subtlety is a word not even whispered here, but savvy is evident everywhere. A spinoff of Sizzler, Buffalo Ranch is all about big hunks of meat, barbecued and otherwise, slabs of ribs, and a few chicken and pasta dishes tucked into a corner of the menu. Portions are large, potatoes are weighed by the pound, and every dinner platter comes with a crisp salad and garlic bread. It's country western dining done cleverly and aiming to please. Best bet is the Bronco Bustin' Sampler plate of half a grilled chicken, a third rack of barbecued ribs, and a half-pound of top sirloin. Some nifty microbrews are available, with Rattlesnake Beer topping the list.

Busalacchi's Ristorante

	Italian/Sicilian
Zone 6 Downtown/Uptown/Central	★★★
3683 Fifth Avenue	Inexpensive/Moderate
298-0119	
	Quality 88 Value B

Reservations:	Recommended
When to go:	Any time, but especially on weekends
Entree range:	$9–22
Payment:	VISA, MC, AMEX, DC, D
Service rating:	★★★
Friendliness rating:	★★★
Parking:	Street, free lot at dinner, valet at lunch
Bar:	Full service
Wine selection:	Good
Dress:	Dressy casual
Disabled access:	No
Customers:	Locals, businesspeople, visitors/tourists
Lunch:	Monday–Friday, 11:30 A.M.–2 P.M.
Dinner:	Sunday–Thursday, 5–9:45 P.M.;
	Friday and Saturday, 5–10:45 P.M.

Atmosphere/setting: It looks and feels like an old house—which it is—with several rooms that are nicely and comfortably appointed with scattered tables cloaked with tablecloths. Sometimes you'll hear squeaks from the floor that only add to the sense of age. There's also an outdoor dining area elevated from the street.

House specialties: Homemade pastas; seafood; veal; chicken.

Other recommendations: Veal chop grilled with rosemary; breaded swordfish stuffed with shrimp and Parmesan cheese; eggplant parmigiana; pasta with fresh broccoli and garlic; pasta and buffalo mozzarella wrapped in eggplant.

Summary & comments: It must be a matter of honor, but at Busalacchi's they simply won't allow a timid flavor past the kitchen door. The emphasis is decidedly Sicilian, and everything is served con gusto which includes caponata, clams, squid, shrimp, eggplant, or whatever. The use of garlic is prolific, and you ought to go with someone you love because after a meal, vampires and mere friends will avoid you for hours. Though Busalacchi's looks a bit formal, it's more akin to a robust picnic. It's also Tommy Lasorda's favorite place, and he makes a point of stopping in when he's in town. A husband and wife team runs the place; he's in the kitchen, and she takes care of the front of the house.

Honors & awards: Gold Medallion Award, Chamber of Commerce Small Business of the Year.

Cafe 222

Zone 6 Downtown/Uptown/Central	California
222 Island Avenue	★★
236-9902	Inexpensive
	Quality 78 Value C

Reservations:	Parties of 6 or more
When to go:	Breakfast
Entree range:	$2–7
Payment:	Cash only
Service rating:	★
Friendliness rating:	★★★
Parking:	Street
Bar:	None
Wine selection:	None
Dress:	Informal
Disabled access:	Yes
Customers:	Locals, businesspeople, visitors/tourists
Breakfast:	Monday–Friday, 7–11:30 A.M.;
	Saturday and Sunday, 7 A.M.–2 P.M.
Lunch:	Every day, 11:30 A.M.–2 P.M.

Atmosphere/setting: A small angular room with a few blond-wood tables and one large booth. Given the limited indoor space, more people eat at the outdoor sidewalk tables.

House specialties: Joe's Special; pumpkin waffles; corn waffles; orange-pecan pancakes; home-baked muffins and scones; home-roasted granola; burger with caramelized onions and goat cheese.

Other recommendations: Hash and eggs; lime and ginger smoked chicken sandwich; meat loaf with garlic mashed potatoes; curried egg salad.

Summary & comments: It's tiny, cute as a button, eclectic as all get out, cheap, fashionable, and a mere two blocks from Horton Plaza. Most of all, it's a diner—an idiosyncratic one to be sure—and one that's the darling of local architects (one of whom designed the place). It's especially popular for breakfast when locals seek it out for the sweet corn waffles or Joe's Special (a frittata of spinach, peppers, potatoes, and eggs), and it's no slouch at lunchtime either, especially when it comes to the cafe burger with caramelized onions and goat cheese.

Cafe Champagne

Zone 1   North County Inland
Thornton Winery,
  32575 Rancho California Road,
  Temecula
(909) 699-0088

California French
★★★
Inexpensive / Moderate

Quality 80   Value C

Reservations:	Recommended
When to go:	After wine tasting
Entree range:	Lunch, $8–17; dinner, $13–22
Payment:	VISA, MC, AMEX
Service rating:	★★
Friendliness rating:	★★★
Parking:	Free lot
Bar:	Limited
Wine selection:	Good
Dress:	Dressy casual, informal
Disabled access:	Yes
Customers:	Locals, visitors / tourists
Brunch:	Sunday, 11 A.M.–4 P.M.
Lunch:	Monday–Saturday, 11 A.M.–4:30 P.M.
Dinner:	Tuesday–Sunday, 5–9:30 P.M.; Monday, closed.

Atmosphere / setting: Little Victorian flourishes are intended to add cozy charm to an L-shaped modern design restaurant where tables and booths are done in light oak and California casual is the dominant mood.

House specialties: Roasted poblano chiles; warm Brie en croûte; carne asada salad; stir-fried chicken and vegetables; seafood cioppino; mesquite-grilled peppercorn chicken; tagliatelle with sea scallops.

Other recommendations: Grilled pork tenderloin with red onion marmalade; penne with oven-roasted tomatoes and broccoli; yellow and white corn chowder; smoked salmon bruschetta; roast veal and smoked mozzarella sandwich.

Summary & comments: Cafe Champagne offers a cool respite after a day of wine tasting in the Temecula Valley, or after just a few taster sips at the Thornton Winery. The food is solidly planted in the middle ground of the California food evolution: ingredients are fresh and combinations are creative, but there's nothing so ingenious to take your breath away. Suggestions are made for food and wine pairings.

Cafe Eleven

Zone 6   Downtown/Uptown/Central
1440 University Avenue
260-8023

California French
★★
Inexpensive/Moderate

Quality 78   Value C

Reservations:	Recommended
When to go:	Dinner
Entree range:	$10–18
Payment:	VISA, MC, AMEX, DC, D
Service rating:	★★
Friendliness rating:	★★★
Parking:	Free lot, street
Bar:	Full service
Wine selection:	Good
Dress:	Dressy casual, informal
Disabled access:	Yes
Customers:	Locals
Dinner:	Tuesday–Saturday, 5 P.M. to closing; Sunday, 5–9 P.M.; Monday, closed.

Atmosphere/setting: Small and intimate, pastel colors, somewhat formal, but the dominant sense is of coziness.

House specialties: Duck with green peppercorn sauce; sweetbreads with port wine and black olive sauce; rack of lamb with rosemary demi-glace.

Other recommendations: Chicken Wellington; fried feta with orange vinaigrette; pork with lemon and capers; red snapper with lime and pecans; pan-fried lamb chops with Dijon crème.

Summary & comments: Cafe Eleven feels like part of someone's house, though it's actually just a small restaurant tucked into the corner of a shopping center. The restaurant is long and linear, there are some tables and a few upholstery-covered banquettes, and the dominant sensation is of a neighborhood gathering spot that's a secret to all but the locals. Menu and preparations tend to be familiar; it's the charm and intimacy of the setting that appeals most of all.

CAFE JAPENGO

Zone 4   Mission Valley and the Mesas
8960 University Center Lane
450-3355

<table>
<tr><td colspan="2">Pacific Rim/Sushi Bar</td></tr>
<tr><td colspan="2">★★★</td></tr>
<tr><td colspan="2">Inexpensive/Moderate</td></tr>
<tr><td>Quality 88</td><td>Value C</td></tr>
</table>

Reservations:	Recommended
When to go:	Any time, but Friday evenings are the densest
Entree range:	$9–22
Payment:	VISA, MC, AMEX, DC, D
Service rating:	★★
Friendliness rating:	★★
Parking:	Fee lot, free lot, valet, street
Bar:	Full service
Wine selection:	Good
Dress:	Dressy casual
Disabled access:	Yes
Customers:	Locals, visitors/tourists
Lunch:	Monday–Friday, 11:30 A.M.–2:30 P.M.; Saturday and Sunday, closed.
Dinner:	Monday–Thursday, 6–10:30 P.M.; Friday and Saturday, 6–11 P.M.; Sunday, 6–10 P.M.
Sushi Bar Only:	Monday–Thursday, 5–11 P.M.; Friday and Saturday, 5 P.M.–midnight; Sunday, 5–10 P.M.

Atmosphere/setting: Arguably one of the most austerely beautiful restaurants in San Diego, Japengo is a mix of Asian aesthetics and Hollywood temperament. Evidence of fine design is everywhere.

House specialties: Whole New Zealand red snapper; slow-roasted duckling with flour tortillas and plum sauce; woked catfish; any dessert.

Other recommendations: Sushi; fried calamari; ten-ingredient fried rice.

Entertainment & amenities: Live blues on Monday nights.

Summary & comments: Offering a mix of Japanese, sometimes Chinese, and occasionally Latin foods, Japengo's menu of a dozen or so items tends to whip cultures together in a wok. Portions are large, plates are beautifully decorated, and the sushi bar is always crowded. For first timers, much of the menu will seem like unfamiliar terrain, but don't hold back. Be sure to question your waitperson freely. The same chef ruled the kitchen for years, but once he left the mania for consistency went, too. Though you'd never guess it, Japengo's is operated by the Hyatt, the hotel that's right across the parking lot.

Honors & awards: *San Diego Magazine,* Best Sushi Bar, four years in a row and Best Japanese, three years; 1995 Gold Medallion, Best Oriental.

Cafe Luna

Italian
★ ★ ★
Inexpensive / Moderate

Quality 81   Value B

Zone 1   North County Inland
11040 Rancho Carmel Drive
673-0077

Reservations:	Recommended
When to go:	Any time
Entree range:	$9–22
Payment:	VISA, MC, AMEX, D
Service rating:	★ ★
Friendliness rating:	★ ★ ★
Parking:	Free lot
Bar:	Limited
Wine selection:	Good
Dress:	Dressy casual, informal
Disabled access:	Yes
Customers:	Locals, businesspeople, visitors / tourists
Dinner:	Monday–Thursday, 5–9 P.M.; Friday and Saturday, 5–9:30 P.M.; Sunday, closed.

Atmosphere / setting: Airy and bistro-like, with rows of small tables set against walls or interior partitions. Mellow lighting. White wood shutters are in the windows, the walls are sponge-painted peach, and the concrete floor has hand-drawn faux cracks so authentic looking most diners think they're from earthquakes. The restaurant is two rooms of about equal size with a bar (which is mostly for looks) in the side room. The calmness of it all seems a little too nice for its shopping center site, which is dominated by a stereo store and a Carls Jr.

House specialties: Di Caesare; fusille unbriaco; rosetta; pollo de la costa; saltimbocca.

Other recommendations: Sicilian salad; pastas—especially the fresh ones—and virtually any dish with shrimp.

Summary & comments: There's an attempt to bridge the distance been Old World Italian and cucina moderna here, but the Old World usually wins. Pasta is the principal offering, though the menu was recently expanded to include more chicken, veal, and seafood entrees. Pasta sauces are purported to have "just a touch" of oil or butter or cream, but the results are often a little too rich and satisfying to believe there's been much restraint. Cafe Luna has the warmth of a family operation (which it is) as well as the expertise of people who've spent their lives in the restaurant business (which they have).

Honors & awards: David Nelson's best 200 restaurants in San Diego.

Cafe on Park

Zone 6   Downtown/Uptown/Central
3831 Park Boulevard
293-7275

American
★★★
Inexpensive
Quality 80   Value B

Reservations:	Only for parties of 5 or more
When to go:	Any time, but especially breakfast or lunch
Entree range:	Breakfast and lunch, $3–8; dinner, $5–13
Payment:	VISA, MC
Service rating:	★
Friendliness rating:	★★
Parking:	Street
Bar:	Microbrewed beers
Wine selection:	Good
Dress:	Informal
Disabled access:	Yes
Customers:	Locals
Breakfast:	Monday–Saturday, 7 A.M.–4 P.M.; Sunday, 8 A.M.–4 P.M.
Lunch:	Tuesday–Saturday, 7 A.M.–5 P.M.; Sunday and Monday, 7 A.M.–4 P.M.
Dinner:	Tuesday–Saturday, 5–11 P.M.; Sunday and Monday, closed.

Atmosphere/setting: Scattered wooden tables with paper placemats, occasionally scattered newspapers, high ceilings, and a wooden lunch counter.

House specialties: Everything is made from scratch—all dressings, roasted turkey, meat loaf, sauces.

Other recommendations: Park Boulevard smoothie with espresso, chocolate, and banana; eggplant sandwich with caramelized onions and Swiss; grilled chicken and Brie on garlic bread; meat loaf and mashed potatoes; spinach tortellini with sun-dried tomatoes and artichokes; pork chops with rosemary and garlic.

Entertainment & amenities: Classic black and white movies shown on movie screen at dinner, including Laurel and Hardy.

Summary & comments: A '90s version of the neighborhood diner for the ever-so-slightly alienated. Locals can comfortably linger over a muffin, coffee, and a copy of one of the dozen local papers and magazines stacked at the front of the restaurant. Or they could dash in for the roast beef and Gorgonzola sandwich and hope someone will pay attention to the need for speed. However laid back service may be, portions are large, sandwiches are creative, and prices are a bargain.

Honors & awards: *San Diego Magazine,* Top Breakfast; Architect Award.

Cafe Pacifica

Zone 6 Downtown/Uptown/Central	Seafood
2414 San Diego Avenue	★★★★
291-6666	Moderate
792-0467	Quality 94 Value C

Reservations:	Recommended
When to go:	Any time
Entree range:	Lunch, $6–9; dinner, $12–18
Payment:	VISA, MC, AMEX, DC, D
Service rating:	★★★
Friendliness rating:	★★
Parking:	Valet, street
Bar:	Full service
Wine selection:	Extensive
Dress:	Dressy casual
Disabled access:	Yes
Customers:	Locals, businesspeople, visitors/tourists
Lunch:	Tuesday–Friday, 11:30 A.M.–2 P.M.; Saturday–Monday, closed.
Dinner:	Every day, 5:30–10 P.M.

Atmosphere/setting: Of the three rooms that make up this restaurant, the upper level with its low roof feels like a gracefully enclosed patio; the lower one with high ceilings seems like the dining room in an elegant home; and the "hidden" one—it's behind a partition—is the most conventional and feels like you're part of a forgotten tribe. The dominant color, like the tablecloths, is a bright white. Tables are closely spaced, and both the twinkly lights and the glassware sparkle.

House specialties: Fresh fish prepared by a variety of cooking techniques.

Other recommendations: Mustard catfish; sea bass.

Summary & comments: From the outside, the look is of an adobe bungalow. Inside is a charming and cosmopolitan setting for one of San Diego's premier fish restaurants. Though it's been around for 15 years, Cafe Pacifica keeps reinventing itself, incorporating what's new and modish with what's proven over time to be successful. Because the Old Town location is off the beaten track—especially for anyone looking for seafood—many customers tend to be fiercely loyal locals or people who've heard of the restaurant by word of mouth. The owner is on the premises every day, and since only fresh fish is served, much of the menu changes daily. There's always a meat entree too.

Honors & awards: Southern California Restaurant Writers Association Gold Award; *Wine Spectator* Award of Excellence.

Caldo Pomodoro

Zone 2   North County Coastal
2907 State Street, Carlsbad
720-9998

Reservations:	Recommended
When to go:	Any time
Entree range:	$6–21
Payment:	VISA, MC, AMEX, DC, D
Service rating:	★★
Friendliness rating:	★★★
Parking:	Free lot, street
Bar:	Wine and beer only
Wine selection:	Good
Dress:	Dressy casual, informal
Disabled access:	Yes
Customers:	Locals, visitors / tourists
Lunch:	Every day, 11 A.M.–4 P.M.
Dinner:	Sunday–Thursday, 4–10 P.M.; Friday and Saturday, 4–11 P.M.

Atmosphere / setting: This corner Italian restaurant, with its densely packed tables covered with red checkered cloths and its neon beer signs, looks like an eatery more likely to exist in a New York or New Jersey neighborhood than in the quaint-bordering-on-cutesy downtown of Carlsbad, California.

House specialties: Seafood (or anything else) with hot tomato sauce, but especially the mixed seafood platter.

Other recommendations: Broccoli with garlic; veal marsala; linguine with clams and mussels; pizza; eggplant parmigiana; Sicilian chicken salad.

Summary & comments: Three little words explain why crowds jam this cozy, brother-and-sister-run restaurant in the Carlsbad Village: It's the sauce. Not just any sauce either. Caldo Pomodoro's rich and spicy tomato sauce is the color of old wine and thick as batter. It's chunky and gutsy and so packed with garlic and jalapeños you smell it long before any dish it covers reaches your table. As the house specialty, the sauce gets ladled over pasta and half the entrees on the menu: calamari, sausage, fresh clams and mussels, chicken, and even steak. There's a mild version of the sauce that's almost as tasty, and you'll detect it on the pizza and in the lasagna. Should you want to go sauceless though, the eggplant parmigiana and the Sicilian chicken salad are excellent.

Honors & awards: Best New Restaurant (two times); Honorable Mention for Best Italian Restaurant in North County.

California Cuisine

California
★★★★
Moderate

Quality 92   Value B

Zone 6   Downtown/Uptown/Central
1027 University Avenue
543-0790

Reservations:	Recommended
When to go:	Any time
Entree range:	$12–18
Payment:	VISA, MC, AMEX, DC, D
Service rating:	★★★
Friendliness rating:	★★★
Parking:	Street
Bar:	None
Wine selection:	Extensive
Dress:	Dressy casual
Disabled access:	Yes
Customers:	Locals, visitors/tourists
Lunch:	Tuesday–Friday, 11 A.M.–5 P.M.; Saturday–Monday, closed.
Dinner:	Tuesday–Sunday, 5–10 P.M.; Monday, closed.

Atmosphere/setting: It's a small room done with chrome and grey and mirrors, with a look that tends toward the modern and slightly austere. The art on the walls is modern, hard-edged, and changes regularly. Out back is a charming patio deck, but the walls of adjacent buildings frame the area and leave no doubt you're in the middle of a city.

House specialties: Crayfish chile relleno with black bean sauce and cilantro cream; pork with wild rice pancakes; black and white sesame seed-seared ahi with hot and sour raspberry sauce.

Other recommendations: Pistachio-crusted calamari steak; capellini with seafood; sea bass poached in tomatillo salsa and Manila clams; New York steak with onion-fennel ragout; curried chicken salad; quail with butternut squash.

Summary & comments: For more than a dozen years, California Cuisine has been nourishing locals with California cooking classics. It's like a gem that's been hidden in the back of your jewelry box: when you come across it, you're amazed you forget such a valuable asset—especially since the menu changes daily. There have been some ups and downs over the years, but the ups are in full swing ever since Chef Chris Walsh became a partner. Presentations are artful or playful or both, and imagination is an ingredient in every dish.

Honors & awards: Southern California Restaurant Writers Association Silver and Gold Awards; *San Diego Home/Garden* Silver Fork Award.

Canton Seafood Restaurant

Zone 7 San Diego East/East County	Chinese/Cantonese
4134 University Avenue	★★
281-6008	Inexpensive
	Quality 75 Value B

Reservations:	Helpful
When to go:	Dinner
Entree range:	$5–14
Payment:	VISA, MC
Service rating:	★★
Friendliness rating:	★
Parking:	Free lot, street
Bar:	None
Wine selection:	Limited
Dress:	Informal
Disabled access:	Yes
Customers:	Locals, ethnic
Open:	Monday–Thursday, 11 A.M.–midnight;
	Friday, 11 A.M.–1 A.M.;
	Saturday, 9 A.M.–1 A.M.;
	Sunday, 9 A.M.–midnight

Atmosphere/setting: It's in the back of a shopping center where the most prominent tenant is a Burger King. The restaurant itself is a large room, newly remodeled, with green commercial carpeting, pink tablecloths, whitewashed wainscotting, and a few Chinese pictures on the wall. It's minimalist, but pleasant.

House specialties: Black bean crab; barbecued lobster with ginger and scallions; preserved Szechuan turnip soup; flounder with green vegetables.

Other recommendations: Dumplings with oyster sauce; squid with shrimp sauce; shredded chicken with bean sprouts; sliced beef with preserved vegetables; fried mixed vegetables.

Summary & comments: It used to be the only place in town to go for crab with black bean sauce, but that's because it was one of the few places that served fresh crab at reasonable prices. There's lots more competition now, but the black bean crab is still excellent. Dim sum is served at lunchtime, but you're better off sticking with the regular menu. The front of the restaurant has enough iron bars to make you think you're entering a maximum security area, but once inside you'll feel totally safe and comfortable.

Carnitas Uruapan

		Mexican
Zone 8	Coronado /	★★
	South Bay / Tijuana	Inexpensive
Boulevard Dias Ordaz 550, Tijuana		
011-52-661-81-6181		Quality 79 Value B

Zone 8   Coronado / South Bay / Tijuana
Paseo de los Heros at Avenida Rodriguez, Tijuana
No phone

Reservations:	Not accepted
When to go:	Evenings
Entree range:	$4–10
Payment:	Cash only
Service rating:	★★
Friendliness rating:	★★
Parking:	Free lot, street
Bar:	Full service
Wine selection:	Limited
Dress:	Informal
Disabled access:	No
Customers:	Locals
Open:	Every day, 8 A.M.–4:30 P.M.

Atmosphere / setting: It's mostly a roadhouse restaurant, and that's what it looks like from the outside. Inside are bright orange picnic tables and other inexpensive decor. Expect it to be smoky—and the later in the evening, the smokier it will get.

House specialties: Carnitas (shredded pork, refried beans, cilantro, onions, salsa—you're served the ingredients and you make it yourself) and cerveza (beer).

Entertainment & amenities: Mariachis perform most weekend evenings.

Summary & comments: Even though it may seem a little formidable on the outside, Carnitas Uruapan has been visited by thousands of tourists and relished by virtually every one of them. There are mostly families in the early evenings and adults exclusively later on. Though it won't be the healthiest or tenderest you'll have, carnitas is what you want. The abandon with which it's made and the setting in which it's served make it taste wonderful. Order carnitas by the kilo (a half-kilo will serve four to six). Though not all of the servers speak English, enough do so that you won't have a hard time ordering. If it's late at night, you'll find the whole experience rambunctious and delightful. To get there, head south on Agua Caliente Boulevard; it's about a quarter-mile south of Agua Caliente Racetrack, on the left side of the road. There's a large sign out front. You can't miss it.

Casa de Bandini

Zone 6 Downtown/Uptown/Central	Mexican
2660 Calhoun	★★
297-8211	Inexpensive/Moderate
	Quality 72 Value C

Reservations:	Not accepted, except for large groups
When to go:	Any time
Entree range:	$6–16
Payment:	VISA, MC, AMEX, DC, D
Service rating:	★★
Friendliness rating:	★
Parking:	Free lot, street
Bar:	Full service
Wine selection:	House
Dress:	Informal
Disabled access:	Yes
Customers:	Locals, businesspeople, visitors/tourists
Open:	Monday–Saturday, 11 A.M.–9 P.M.; Sunday, 10 A.M.–9 P.M.

Atmosphere/setting: A large restored hacienda made up of several rooms and a courtyard. The decor is bright and flashy, with hot tropical colors, splashing fountains, and the sound of mariachis.

House specialties: Sopa Azteca; Mexican corn soup; chicken fajita salad; enchiladas suizas; fish tacos; tequila lime shrimp; arroz con pollo; burrito carnitas.

Other recommendations: Seafood tostada; avocado omelet; crab enchiladas; tamales; fajitas; seafood chimichanga.

Entertainment & amenities: Live music seven nights a week.

Summary & comments: There's not much on the menu at Casa de Bandini that'll make you swoon with delight, but the environment will have you olé-ing instantly. It's unquestionably the place to encounter the Myth of Old Mexico, especially for folks who've never been south of the border. More than anything else, Casa de Bandini is a triumph of splendid decor—and that makes it genuinely ideal for visitors and groups of celebrants. If the day is sunny, be sure to sit in the outdoor courtyard and get comfortable with a birdbath-sized margarita as you get lulled into tranquility by sounds of water spraying from the fountain. Food at the Sunday brunch is actually quite good, and that's also when the mariachis stroll by your table. It's a terrific place to take younger children.

Honors & awards: San Diego Restaurant Association Gold Medallion Awards.

Cheese Shop

	American
Zone 3 La Jolla	★★
2165 Avenida de la Playa	Inexpensive
459-3921	
Zone 6 Downtown/Uptown/Central	Quality 78 Value C
401 G Street	
232-2303	

Reservations:	Not accepted
When to go:	Any time
Entree range:	$5–7
Payment:	VISA, MC
Service rating:	★★
Friendliness rating:	★★★
Parking:	Street
Bar:	Limited
Wine selection:	Limited
Dress:	Informal
Disabled access:	Yes
Customers:	Locals, businesspeople
Breakfast/Lunch:	Monday–Saturday, 8 A.M.–6 P.M.;
	Sunday, 8 A.M.–5 P.M. (La Jolla);
	Monday–Friday, 8 A.M.–5 P.M.;
	Saturday and Sunday, 10 A.M.–4 P.M. (G Street)

Atmosphere/setting: A large room with colorful tables and a sandwich counter. It's a slightly hipper version of the standard sandwich shop.

House specialties: Roasted pork loin with Jack and avocado; spicy Dijon chicken salad; roast beef—all made on the premises.

Other recommendations: Smoked salmon with cream cheese, onions, and capers; hot corned beef, pastrami, and Swiss; home-roasted turkey breast; red-skin potato salad.

Summary & comments: All the sandwiches and their various elements are made on the premises. What you get are often called "honest sandwiches" because they're filled with quality ingredients provided in ample—but not theatrical—quantity. As the name implies, the options for cheese are broad, but so are choices in meats and salads. The aroma of freshly baked cookies and muffins pervades the place. And though it's low on decor, there's an earnestness about it that makes it an ideal stop-off for coffee, juice, or an espresso. You can sit, sip, eat your sandwich, read the paper, and be left blessedly alone. It's also a favorite for the downtown working crowd.

Chez Odette

Zone 6   Downtown/Uptown/Central
3614 Fifth Avenue
299-1000

Deli	
★★★	
Inexpensive	
Quality 85	Value B

Reservations:	Not accepted
When to go:	Any time
Entree range:	$5–8
Payment:	Cash only
Service rating:	★★★
Friendliness rating:	★★★
Parking:	Street
Bar:	To go only
Wine selection:	To go only
Dress:	Informal
Disabled access:	No
Customers:	Locals
Breakfast:	Monday–Friday, 8:30–10:30 A.M.; Saturday and Sunday, closed.
Lunch:	Monday–Friday, 11 A.M.–3 P.M.; Saturday and Sunday, closed.

Atmosphere/setting: It looks like a deli crossed with a home kitchen. It is mostly a deli, but there are a few tables and a counter where you can eat.

House specialties: Hot entrees change daily. Most days there are sandwiches, including garlic saucisson; baked turkey, ham, roast beef; eggplant Parmesan; beef bourguignonne; quiches; Grand Marnier chocolate cake; apple tarte.

Other recommendations: Almond pound cake; paupiette of beef or chicken; avocado stuffed with shrimp.

Summary & comments: A mom-and-pop shop. She's the cook and he's the pastry chef, and both of them were formally trained in Europe. Many of the customers are regulars, and many drop in as much for conversation as for Odette Sprenger's home cooking. A good deal of the business is catering, and it's unusual in that Chez Odette will handle both very small and very large jobs.

Chilango's Mexico City Grill

Regional Mexican	
★★★★	
Inexpensive	
Quality 90 Value A	

Zone 6   Downtown/Uptown/Central
142 University Avenue
294-8646

Reservations:	Not accepted
When to go:	Any time
Entree range:	$4–7
Payment:	Cash
Service rating:	★
Friendliness rating:	★★
Parking:	Street
Bar:	None
Wine selection:	None
Dress:	Informal
Disabled access:	Yes
Customers:	Locals
Breakfast:	Monday–Friday, 8–11:30 A.M.;
	Saturday and Sunday, 8 A.M.–1 P.M.

Atmosphere/setting: Brightly decorated, tiny and tidy, this is a store front with about six tables inside and an equal number out on the street. The look is strictly in the fast-food mode.

House specialties: Carne asada or pork loin torta; Mexican vegetable quesadilla; seafood huarache; chicken and avocado salad.

Other recommendations: Pico de gallo fruit salad; charro beans; cafe de olla; carne asada and eggs; shredded jerk beef with salsa ranchero; chile relleno quesadilla; mango mousse.

Summary & comments: Chilango's is glorious proof there is still something new under el sol. It takes us away from tacos and combination plates and teaches that delicious and unusual regional Mexican cooking is found not just in private homes and stately restaurants but in little more than sidewalk grills. It also teaches us that huaraches are not only for feet. The food is so good and so fascinating, it's worth tolerating the erratic service.

Chino

Southwestern/Sushi Bar

★★

Moderate/Expensive

Quality 79   Value D

Zone 6   Downtown/Uptown/Central
919 Fourth Avenue
231-9240

Reservations:	Accepted, but essential on weekends
When to go:	Any time
Entree range:	$8–21
Payment:	VISA, MC, AMEX, DC, D
Service rating:	★★
Friendliness rating:	★★
Parking:	Valet, street
Bar:	Full service
Wine selection:	Extensive
Dress:	Dressy casual
Disabled access:	Yes
Customers:	Locals, visitors/tourists
Lunch:	Monday–Friday, 11:30 A.M.–2:30 P.M.; Saturday and Sunday, closed.
Dinner:	Tuesday and Wednesday, 5:30–10 P.M.; Thursday–Saturday, 5:30–10:30 P.M.; Sunday and Monday, closed.

Atmosphere/setting: Chino is the restaurant portion of an enormous entertainment center in the Gaslamp called "E Street Alley." The restaurant, Chino, is the most lavish of all the rooms. It has high ceilings, brick walls, concrete floors, and it's furnished with black granite tables, tropical flowers, and soft lighting. Very dramatic, very supper club, very hip.

House specialties: Pecan-smoked prawn roll with wok-charred basil; jasmine tea–smoked Chilean sea bass; spicy smoked jalapeño-cured salmon roll; seared rare ahi tuna; seared and woked lamb chops.

Other recommendations: Scallop ceviche gazpacho; duck and cheese spring rolls; pan-fried catfish with smoked corn crust; vegetables kung pao.

Entertainment & amenities: Besides the restaurants, E Street Alley includes a few bars, a huge dance hall, a chill-out parlor, and a billiards area. Weekend nights are the busiest time, but if you have dinner at Chino's, there's no cover charge for the dance hall and you don't have to wait in line to get in.

Summary & comments: The food is all about fusion cookery, which is sometimes so exotic and dizzying, you're certain you've stopped at Fantasy Island. If anything comes with a preparation that seems too over the edge (like the coffee-bean sauce that accompanies the lamb), ask the kitchen to serve it on the side.

Cilantro's

Southwestern

★★★

Inexpensive / Moderate

Quality 84   Value C

Zone 2   North County Coastal
3702 Via de la Valle 101, Del Mar
259-8777

Reservations:	Recommended
When to go:	Any time
Entree range:	$11–21
Payment:	VISA, MC, AMEX
Service rating:	★★
Friendliness rating:	★★
Parking:	Free lot, valet
Bar:	Full service
Wine selection:	Extensive
Dress:	Dressy casual
Disabled access:	Yes
Customers:	Locals, businesspeople, visitors / tourists
Brunch:	Sunday, 10:30 A.M.–3 P.M.
Lunch:	Monday–Saturday, 11:30 A.M.–3 P.M.
Dinner:	Monday–Thursday, 5–10:30 P.M.;
	Friday and Saturday, 5–11 P.M.;
	Sunday, 5–9:30 P.M.

Atmosphere / setting: Familiar Southwestern setting with pale pastels, bleached woods, and some very dull commercial art.

House specialties: Baby-back ribs with peanut habanero sauce; chile-crusted sea scallop tostada; chicken and wild mushroom risotto; grilled swordfish with anasazi bean ragout; spit-roasted duck; barbecued pork tenderloin with corn relish; marinated carne asada with wild mushroom salsa.

Other recommendations: Tamales: cranberry-apple, black bean with garlic cream, chicken and achiote; barbecued quail with sweet potato nests.

Summary & comments: Driving inland from the coast, just when you think you've traveled beyond the commercial area, you'll come to a wide space in the road near polo fields and some of the most expensive homes in the county. Suddenly there's Cilantro's, where the well-heeled wind down in comfort. Though it was among the first restaurants in the area to feature Sante Fe–style foods with a bite, Cilantro's has moved to a milder place where the emphasis is more on decorator Southwestern—mild flavors with visual flourish. Still, whether you're looking around the table or out the window, the views are sensational.

Honors & awards: *Entertainer,* Best Margarita 1991–1995; Southern California Restaurant Writers Association Southwestern Gold Award.

Cindy Black's

Zone 3   La Jolla
5721 La Jolla Boulevard
456-6299

Reservations:	Recommended
When to go:	Any time
Entree range:	$9–22
Payment:	VISA, MC, AMEX, DC, D
Service rating:	★★★
Friendliness rating:	★★★
Parking:	Street, valet on Friday and Saturday
Bar:	Full service
Wine selection:	Extensive
Dress:	Dressy casual
Disabled access:	Yes
Customers:	Locals, visitors/tourists
Dinner:	Monday–Saturday, 5:30–10 P.M.; Sunday, 5–8 P.M.

Atmosphere/setting: The restaurant's dark facade and elaborate entry vestibule are rather formidable, but once inside, the several rooms that make up the dining area take on a homey sensibility. In an attempt to overcome the age and slightly threadbare quality of the room, lots of bright and even cheeky colors have been applied. Bold art adorns the walls.

House specialties: Portobello mushrooms; house hors d'oeuvres plate; grilled duck "two ways"; imported Dover sole; Provençal chicken stew; raspberry crêpes.

Other recommendations: Fritto misto of shrimp, calamari, and sweetbreads; spaghetti and white beans in chianti.

Summary & comments: The sense of personality is very strong, as if you're having dinner at the home of a friend who is an exceptional and distinctive cook. Food is done not so much with a flourish as with substance. While the menu changes with the seasons, the emphasis is always on hearty home cooking. Proprietor and chef Cindy Black once headed the kitchen of San Diego's most sophisticated and elegant hotel restaurant. Now she and her husband—also a chef—run their own place and emphasize comfort, both in setting and food. There's a Monday-to-Friday three-course fixed price special at $13.

Honors & awards: DiRona 1992–1995; Southern California Restaurant Writers, three-star rating.

Claim Jumper

Zone 1 North County Inland
12384 Carmel Mountain Road
485-8370

Zone 2 North County Coastal
5958 Avenida Encinas, Carlsbad
431-0889

Zone 7 San Diego East/East County
5500 Grossmont Center Drive, La Mesa
469-3927

American	
★★★	
Inexpensive/Moderate	
Quality 85	Value A

Reservations:	Not accepted
When to go:	Go early or late to beat the crowds
Entree range:	$6–22
Payment:	VISA, MC, AMEX, DC, D
Service rating:	★★
Friendliness rating:	★★★★
Parking:	Free lot
Bar:	Full service
Wine selection:	Good
Dress:	Informal
Disabled access:	Yes
Customers:	Locals, businesspeople, tourists/visitors
Lunch:	Every day, 11 A.M.–5 P.M.
Dinner:	Every day, 5 P.M.–closing

Atmosphere/setting: Imagine a gussied-up version of the bunk house from *Seven Brides for Seven Brothers.* This huge restaurant is divided into a number of smaller serving areas, but everywhere is dark wood, high ceilings, and newly minted Victoriana mixed with some of the genuine articles.

House specialties: Baby-back ribs; rotisseried chicken; 26-ounce prime rib; fresh fish; woodfired pizzas.

Other recommendations: Broiled pork loin chops; chicken pot pie; onion rings (get the thin ones rather than the thick cut, which look like Madonna's bra); vegetable stack sandwich; salad bar; spinach lasagna.

Summary & comments: Huge portions are the hallmark of this Southern California chain. Vegetable platters approximate truck farming operations and hunks of chicken, meat, and fish can sometimes overwhelm. Most of the food is quite good, though I'd stay away from the roasted turkey supper, which has the taste of leftovers. Claim Jumper is staffed with servers as cheery as the guides at Disneyland but with serious kitchen staff who turn out impressively good food.

The Corvette Diner, Bar & Grill

<table>
<tr><td>American</td></tr>
<tr><td>★★</td></tr>
<tr><td>Inexpensive</td></tr>
<tr><td>Quality 79   Value C</td></tr>
</table>

Zone 6   Downtown/Uptown/Central
3946 Fifth Avenue
542-1001

Reservations:	Not accepted
When to go:	Any time
Entree range:	$5–9
Payment:	VISA, MC, AMEX, DC, D
Service rating:	★★
Friendliness rating:	★★★★
Parking:	Valet, street
Bar:	Full service
Wine selection:	House
Dress:	Informal
Disabled access:	Yes
Customers:	Locals, visitors/tourists
Open:	Sunday–Thursday, 11 A.M.–11 P.M.;
	Friday and Saturday, 11 A.M.–midnight

Atmosphere/setting: A souped-up vision of the 1950s, all innocent and carefree, with leatherette and chrome booths and bold and colorful decor that includes neon and other road signs of the period, well-amplified music, and a highly polished and pedestal-mounted car in the middle of the room.

House specialties: Beef, turkey, and veggie burgers; meat loaf; chicken-fried steak; giant salads.

Other recommendations: Salmon burger; tuna cheddar melt; calamari sandwich; Philly steak sandwich; chili fries; malts and shakes.

Entertainment & amenities: The "World Famous Dancing Corvette Crew." Disc jockeys seven nights a week take requests and play dedications. Magic Mike every Tuesday and Wednesday. Entertainers on Friday and Saturday nights.

Summary & comments: One of the first '50s-style diners in San Diego, it's still the most clever, successful, and crowded. Servers are a mite too chummy for their own good, like when they sit down next to you while taking your order. The best menu items are the ones you have nothing else to compare to, like the chicken-fried steak or the vegetarian lasagna. Get either one with a chocolate malt and you can make a return visit to adolescent heaven. It's all a kick, perfect for kids and 50th birthdays. But arrive early since the wait can be a long one, especially at dinnertime and on weekends.

CREST CAFE

Zone 6   Downtown/Uptown/Central
425 Robinson Avenue
295-2510

Reservations:	Only for parties of 5 or more
When to go:	Any time
Entree range:	$4–13
Payment:	VISA, MC, AMEX, D
Service rating:	★★
Friendliness rating:	★★
Parking:	Street; validated parking on 4th Avenue
Bar:	Beer
Wine selection:	Good
Dress:	Informal
Disabled access:	Yes
Customers:	Locals
Open:	Monday–Friday, 7 A.M.–11:30 P.M.;
	Saturday, 7 A.M.–midnight;
	Sunday, 7 A.M.–1 A.M.

Atmosphere/setting: The look is small-town coffee shop, with a few booths and closely spaced tables. Formica is here and there.

House specialties: Nine types of burgers; grilled vegetarian sandwich; jalapeño chicken salad; homemade soups and desserts.

Other recommendations: Fish and chips; hot chicken salad; vegetarian chili; turkey and Brie on grilled sourdough.

Summary & comments: If the Crest were anywhere else, it would probably be unremarkable. But since it's in Hillcrest—a gathering spot for the gay and lesbian communities and straight singles with disposable incomes—the Crest is a de facto neighborhood nucleus, a place where folks of all dispositions and intentions can read the paper undisturbed at Sunday breakfast—or check out the crowd that most other diners also seem to be checking out. When things get busy, the kitchen can get a little haphazard, and normally terrific homemade potato chips may come up soft and grease-drenched. Fresh fruit salad is available as a substitute for most side orders, and vegetarian food requests are as normal as another pierced eyebrow.

Honors & awards: *Union-Tribune* Best Burger/Onion Loaf.

CROCE'S RESTAURANT

		California
Zone 6 Downtown/Uptown/Central		★★★★
802 Fifth Avenue		Moderate
233-4355		Quality 90 Value B

Reservations:	Recommended
When to go:	Dinner
Entree range:	$12–22
Payment:	VISA, MC, AMEX, DC, D
Service rating:	★★★
Friendliness rating:	★★★
Parking:	Valet, street
Bar:	Full service
Wine selection:	Good
Dress:	Dressy casual
Disabled access:	Yes
Customers:	Locals, businesspeople, visitors/tourists
Dinner:	Every day, 5 P.M.–midnight

Atmosphere/setting: A familiar white tablecloth environment in an older building, with an upstairs dining area that's not quite as connected with what's going on as the downstairs area. The feeling is slightly clubby because of the Victorian building that houses the restaurant, but there's a distinctively upbeat edge to it all.

House specialties: Alaskan halibut; salmon; swordfish; steak; rack of lamb.

Entertainment & amenities: Live jazz nightly, free admission with purchase of dinner entree.

Summary & comments: Ingrid Croce runs her namesake restaurant on the busiest corner of the Gaslamp Quarter. She's the widow (now remarried) of singer Jim Croce, and the mother of rising star blues/jazz singer/pianist A. J. Croce. At last count, Ms. Croce ran four eating and drinking establishments all set in a row on Fifth Avenue. Music with an irresistible beat pulses out of at least two of the places, but her casually elegant dinner restaurant feels like you're in the eye of the storm. Though the sense of tranquility will fray a bit especially on the hectic weekends, the deliberate and carefully prepared food returns a sense of calm. It's all crafted with a light touch and subtle flavorings, and the textures of everything—fish, meats, or poultry—are buttery and warming. Many of the diners—people in their 30s, 40s, and 50s—will move next door for more music once dinner is over.

Honors & awards: San Diego Restaurant Association, Best Late Night Dining, Best Bar in San Diego.

D. Z. Aiken's

Zone 7   San Diego East/East County
Alvarado Plaza, 6930 Alvarado Road
265-0218

<table>
<tr><td>New York–Style Deli</td></tr>
<tr><td>★★★</td></tr>
<tr><td>Inexpensive</td></tr>
<tr><td>Quality 80   Value B</td></tr>
</table>

Reservations:	Accepted only for 6 or more
When to go:	Any time, but especially breakfast/brunch
Entree range:	$7–15
Payment:	VISA, MC
Service rating:	★★★★
Friendliness rating:	★★★
Parking:	Free lot, street
Bar:	Limited
Wine selection:	House
Dress:	Informal
Disabled access:	Yes
Customers:	Locals, businesspeople, ethnic
Open:	Sunday–Thursday, 7 A.M.–9 P.M.;
	Friday and Saturday, 7 A.M.–11 P.M.

Atmosphere/setting: It has the look and smell of what it is, a Southern California deli. There's room after room of grey leatherette booths and formica-topped tables, and constant frantic movement by waitstaff, bussers, and small children looking for the bathrooms.

House specialties: Lox; knishes; bagels; Reuben sandwiches; stuffed cabbage.

Other recommendations: Scrambled lox, eggs, and onions; matzo brei; chicken liver and onions; knockwurst plate; chopped liver on rye.

Summary & comments: In every food poll taken in San Diego, residents lament the absence of a good Jewish deli. But it's not really absence that's the issue, it's paucity. D. Z. Aiken's is a model for what's so scarce. Started years ago by a husband-and-wife team near San Diego State University, it was a small place in a town starved for corned beef sandwiches and matzo ball soup. Reaction was so good, the deli expanded when the shop next door became available. Then it expanded again. Then again. Now the Aiken's deli takes up half the shopping center (which they eventually bought). Breakfasts are especially good, sandwiches are appropriately enormous, and the rye bread is absolutely the best in town. A bakery and deli counter are set up for takeout.

Honors & awards: Golden Medallion, California Restaurant Association; People's Choice, *San Diego Magazine;* Silver Fork, *San Diego Home/Garden Magazine.*

98

Daily's Fit and Fresh

California/Health Food
★★★★
Inexpensive

Quality 90   Value B

Zone 4   Mission Valley and the Mesas
8915 Towne Center Drive
453-1112

Reservations:	Not accepted
When to go:	Any time
Entree range:	$5–7
Payment:	VISA, MC
Service rating:	★★
Friendliness rating:	★★
Parking:	Free lot at the Towne Center location; street parking on Fifth Avenue
Bar:	None
Wine selection:	None
Dress:	Informal
Disabled access:	Yes
Customers:	Locals, businesspeople
Open:	Monday–Saturday, 10:30 A.M.–9 P.M.; Sunday, 11 A.M.–8 P.M.

Atmosphere/setting: Modern, hard-edged, and highly architectonic, Daily's interior design is distinctly Japanese, with its overhead laminated beams and intersecting planes. Blond wood and grey formica are used throughout. Booths are good-looking but fairly uncomfortable since there's no padding on the bench-style seat. The tables and chairs in the middle of the room offer less privacy, but more comfort.

House specialties: All menu items have under ten grams of fat. Tortilla bean soup; chicken gumbo; grilled eggplant and bell pepper on sourdough; white bean and tuna salad; three-bean chili; oatmeal raisin cookies.

Other recommendations: Baja pasta salad; Thai noodle salad; vegetable burger; grilled chicken breast; fish taco pita pocket; Cajun catfish.

Summary & comments: Tasty health food is usually an oxymoron, but Daily's is vibrant proof it's possible to prepare ingenious, satisfying, and even luscious food that's implausibly healthy. Actually, Daily's gives health food a good name. It's the brainchild of a local heart surgeon working with a restaurateur. Sprouts and other hallmarks of standard vegetariana are kept to a minimum, and the emphasis instead is on fresh herbs and clever food combos.

Honors & awards: Best Healthy Restaurant, Channel 8; *San Diego Home/Garden Magazine,* Silver Fork Award 1993, 1994.

Delicias

Zone 2 North County Coastal	California French
6106 Paseo Delicias, Rancho Santa Fe	★★★
756-8000	Moderate/Expensive
	Quality 80 Value D

Reservations:	Recommended
When to go:	Any time
Entree range:	Lunch, $10–12; dinner, $16–26
Payment:	VISA, MC, AMEX, DC, D
Service rating:	★★
Friendliness rating:	★★★
Parking:	Street
Bar:	Full service
Wine selection:	Extensive
Dress:	Dressy casual
Disabled access:	Yes
Customers:	Locals, visitors/tourists
Lunch:	Tuesday–Saturday, 11 A.M.–2 P.M.; Sunday and Monday, closed.
Dinner:	Tuesday–Thursday, Sunday, 6–10 P.M.; Friday and Saturday, 6 P.M.–midnight

Atmosphere/setting: Country French for the gentry. There's an indoor and outdoor seating area; the outdoors is pleasant, but the indoors is sumptuous. Inside are wood-trimmed upholstered chairs and banquettes, French print tablecloths, tapestry and mirrors lining creamy walls, polished marble floors, and very high ceilings. For ladies, the ever-essential purse stool is provided.

House specialties: Duck on watercress with mango port sauce; swordfish with papaya chutney; veal with mushroom risotto; pastas; pizza.

Other recommendations: Blackened tuna; filet mignon; soft-shell crabs with pasta.

Summary & comments: Delicias has a faithful following, though most of it appears to be based on the lovely setting rather than extraordinary food. The menu is small, presentations are pleasing, and service is extremely attentive. The many hard surfaces tend to bounce and amplify sounds, so even though the restaurant is not large, it can be noisy when only half the tables are filled.

D'Lish Gourmet Pasta and Pizza

	Italian / Pizza
	★★★
	Inexpensive
	Quality 80 Value B

Zone 3   La Jolla
7514 Girard Avenue
459-8118

Zone 8   Coronado / South Bay / Tijuana
386 East H Street, Chula Vista
585-1371

Reservations:	For large groups only
When to go:	Any time
Entree range:	$6–9
Payment:	VISA, MC, AMEX, D
Service rating:	★★
Friendliness rating:	★★
Parking:	Street, free lot depending on location
Bar:	Limited
Wine selection:	Limited
Dress:	Informal
Disabled access:	Yes
Customers:	Locals
Open:	Sunday–Thursday, 11:30 A.M.–10 P.M.; Friday and Saturday, 11:30 A.M.–11 P.M. (La Jolla); Sunday–Tuesday, 11:30 A.M.–9 P.M.; Wednesday–Saturday, 11:30 A.M.–10 P.M. (Chula Vista)

Atmosphere / setting: The La Jolla branch is modern and spiffy, mostly the consequence of the failed but fashionable Italian restaurant that last occupied the site. There's full service at both locations.

House specialties: Pizzas: barbecued chicken, Hawaiian, pesto, wild mushroom, grilled vegetable. Rotisserie chicken; Caesar salads; chicken fettuccine; fresh tomatoes with angelhair pasta and goat cheese.

Other recommendations: Lasagna; black bean and chili burger; Chinese chicken salad.

Summary & comments: Large portions of pretty good food is what D'Lish is all about. Order one salad and one pizza as lunch or dinner for two and you'll be more than satisfied. Chicken is usually good, burgers are fine, but pasta tends to be only so-so.

Dick's Last Resort

Zone 6   Downtown/Uptown/Central
345 Fourth Avenue
231-9100

	American
	★
	Inexpensive/Moderate
	Quality 68 Value C

Reservations:	For parties of 8 or more
When to go:	Evenings, weekends
Entree range:	Lunch, $3–9; dinner, $9–15
Payment:	VISA, MC, AMEX, DC, D
Service rating:	★★
Friendliness rating:	★
Parking:	Street, fee lot
Bar:	Full service
Wine selection:	House
Dress:	Informal
Disabled access:	Yes
Customers:	Locals, visitors/tourists
Lunch:	Monday–Saturday, 11 A.M.–4 P.M.; Sunday, closed.
Dinner:	Every day, 4 P.M.–midnight

Atmosphere/setting: Outdoors is a large and comfortable courtyard, and indoors is a large and woody barroom.

House specialties: Beef ribs; pork ribs; barbecue chicken.

Other recommendations: Fried catfish sandwich; boiled shrimp; cheeseburger; rib-eye steak; teriyaki chicken sandwich; grilled shrimp Caesar salad.

Entertainment & amenities: Live entertainment nightly.

Summary & comments: As the San Diego link in a Texas chain, Dick's promises a lively and periodically rowdy time—and then does all it can to promote it. Waitresses are bold, though sometimes they go way over the top in their Don't Mess with Me Buster attitudes. There's a lot of food sold here, but that's really not the point. Beer and cheer attract a mostly younger crowd, and the sound level rises as the evening wears on. What's impossible to resist, though, is the inordinately clever writing that finds its way into ads and menus. Dick's is the self-proclaimed "Shame of the Gaslamp Quarter," and of their salads they say, "People bitched so much we added 'em on."

Dobson's

	California French
Zone 6 Downtown/Uptown/Central	★★★
956 Broadway Circle	Moderate
231-6771	
	Quality 88 Value C

Reservations:	Recommended
When to go:	Any time
Entree range:	Lunch, $5–12; dinner, $12–20
Payment:	VISA, MC, AMEX, DC
Service rating:	★★★
Friendliness rating:	★★
Parking:	Street, valet after 5 P.M.
Bar:	Full service
Wine selection:	Extensive
Dress:	Dressy casual
Disabled access:	Yes
Customers:	Locals, businesspeople, visitors/tourists
Lunch:	Monday–Friday, 11:30 A.M.–3 P.M.; Saturday and Sunday, closed.
Dinner:	Monday–Wednesday, 5:30–10 P.M.; Thursday–Saturday, 5:30–11 P.M.; Sunday, closed.

Atmosphere/setting: A very narrow room with a long bar along one wall and a few tables opposite. Upstairs is a small dining room with very closely spaced tables. It's all serious, urban, and very downtown.

House specialties: Mussel bisque; sweetbreads; confit of duck; herb-crusted rack of lamb.

Other recommendations: Steelhead salmon in puff pastry; Chilean sea bass; pepper-crusted venison loin; cowboy steak.

Summary & comments: Dobson's has had so many ups and downs it's hard to keep track. Still, a down for Dobson's could be an up for most other places. The food is consistently good, though not as predictably wowing as it once was. Yet for local color and flavor, you can't beat Dobson's bar, bar burger, or the deservedly famous mussel bisque. One might be tempted to call Dobson's a drinking wo/man's bar and grill, but it's more than that. It's a local institution where movers and shakers still bend an elbow and linger wistfully over platters of some of downtown's choicest bistro fare.

Honors & awards: Best Bar, Best Business Lunch, Best Late Night Dining, *San Diego Magazine* Readers' Poll.

DOMENIC'S RISTORANTE

	Italian
	★★
	Inexpensive
	Quality 73 Value B

Zone 1   North County Inland
12719 Poway Road, Poway
748-9563

Reservations:	Recommended
When to go:	Any time
Entree range:	$6–17
Payment:	VISA, MC, AMEX, DC, D
Service rating:	★★
Friendliness rating:	★★★
Parking:	Free lot, street
Bar:	None
Wine selection:	Good
Dress:	Informal
Disabled access:	Yes
Customers:	Locals, businesspeople
Open:	Sunday–Thursday, 11 A.M.–9 P.M.;
	Friday and Saturday, 11 A.M.–10 P.M.

Atmosphere / setting: A big room, cheerfully and casually decorated in greens and reds with blond wood accents. The sense is of a slightly ennobled coffee shop.

House specialties: Fried calamari; veal scaloppine with garlic, ham, and capers; penne alla putanesca; potato gnocchi; chicken marsala.

Other recommendations: Linguine with clams; chicken Gorgonzola; ravioli with bacon, onions, and peas.

Entertainment & amenities: Traditional Italian background music.

Summary & comments: Though the food only occasionally rises above average, Domenic's is appealing because of its large portions and the opportunity for families to have an inexpensive and easygoing evening out. It's a near-perfect place for taking little kids and seniors because the commotion is neighborly and affable, and the seasonings are very mild.

El Bizcocho

Zone 1   North County Inland
Rancho Bernardo Inn,
  17550 Bernardo Oaks Drive
487-1611

Continental
★★★★★
Expensive
Quality 97   Value C

Reservations:	Recommended
When to go:	Dinner
Entree range:	Dinner, $17–29; brunch, $19.50
Payment:	VISA, MC, AMEX, DC
Service rating:	★★★★
Friendliness rating:	★★
Parking:	Free lot
Bar:	Full service
Wine selection:	Extensive
Dress:	Dressy, business attire
Disabled access:	Yes
Customers:	Locals, visitors/tourists
Brunch:	Sunday, 10 A.M.–1 P.M.
Dinner:	Sunday–Thursday, 6–9:30 P.M.;
	Friday and Saturday, 6–10 P.M.

Atmosphere/setting: A large room that's been made moody, lit softly, and filled with generously sized tables. The Early California theme that permeates the rest of the Inn seeps into the restaurant and takes on considerable elegance. Understatement is the order of the day.

House specialties: Foie gras with red currants; marinated shrimp; pork loin with hot and sour black bean sauce; swordfish with basil fettuccine; whitefish in potato crust.

Other recommendations: Sautéed ostrich with shiitake mushrooms; tortellini with eggplant, artichokes, and tomato; butternut squash soup.

Summary & comments: As the main dining room in the lovely Rancho Bernardo Inn, El Bizcocho is a throwback to the era of formal and elegant dining strongly rooted in the classics. This is the place for waiters in tuxedos, snails in garlic butter, simply and superbly grilled meats and fish, and an astonishing wine list. Sunday brunch is legendary and the Mother's Day brunch is the justifiably glorious granddaddy of such events; it's an extravaganza that's an unqualified Must Do. A half-dozen times a year, El Bizcocho organizes wine dinners that feel like convivial evenings at Versailles. They're full of frills and drama, serious but lavish food and drink, and plenty of pampering.

El Indio

	Mexican
	★★
	Inexpensive
	Quality 72 Value B

Zone 5   Mission Bay and Beaches
4120 Mission Boulevard
272-8226

Zone 6   Downtown/Uptown/Central
3695 India Street
299-0333

Zone 6   Downtown/Uptown/Central
409 F Street
239-8151

Reservations:	Not accepted
When to go:	Any time
Entree range:	$2–5
Payment:	VISA, MC, D
Service rating:	★★
Friendliness rating:	★★
Parking:	Free lot, street
Bar:	None
Wine selection:	House
Dress:	Informal
Disabled access:	Yes
Customers:	Locals
Open:	Every day, 7 A.M.–9 P.M.

Atmosphere/setting: About a notch-and-a-half above the merely basic, with a deli-like counter where you place orders and a large seating area where there are lots of booths.

House specialties: Tortilla chips; taquitos; chickichanga; carne asada burrito.

Other recommendations: Vegetarian tamale; huevos con chorizo; shredded beef tostada; green enchilada; nachos deluxe.

Summary & comments: El Indio is the wildly popular prototype for virtually all other fast-food Mexican restaurants in the area. Its reputation is based on serving lots of hearty, reasonably authentic food at plausible prices. The original location on India Street has an outdoor seating area that feels like you're picnicking on a traffic median, but how often do you get that chance? Pete Wilson, both as Governor and Senator, frequently has parties catered by El Indio. But the real heart of El Indio is in its tortilla chips. They're phenomenal, spectacular, outrageous—so good in fact that people buy them by the box and ship them around the country. These tortilla chips also make a perfect take-home memento.

El Tecolote

Zone 4   Mission Valley and the Mesas
6110 Friars Road
295-2087

Regional Mexican

★ ★ ★

Inexpensive

Quality 82   Value B

Reservations:	Recommended
When to go:	Any time
Entree range:	$4–11
Payment:	VISA, MC, AMEX, DC, D
Service rating:	★ ★ ★
Friendliness rating:	★ ★
Parking:	Free lot, street
Bar:	Full service
Wine selection:	House
Dress:	Informal
Disabled access:	Yes
Customers:	Locals, businesspeople
Open:	Monday–Saturday, 11 A.M.–10 P.M.; Sunday, 4–9 P.M.

Atmosphere / setting: Three rooms in a small shopping center, two of which are filled with formica-topped tables and an overpowering sense of brown. The third room, also brown and formica-ed, is a bar and billiards area. It's all hospitable and low key.

House specialties: Chicken soup; pastel Azteca; carne asada burrito; enchiladas verdes; stuffed zucchini; stuffed cauliflower; carnitas; chile verde; beef tongue Veracruz.

Other recommendations: Breaded steak; chiles rellenos; shredded beef and eggs.

Summary & comments: A family-run operation where you won't find ordinary cooking because the emphasis is on regional Mexican foods. Year after year, the carne asada burrito remains a standout, the best of its kind in a town full of carne asada aspirants. If the day or night is even barely cool, or if you're feeling a little low, or whatever reason you can come up with, jump at the chance to order the chicken soup. This Mexican version of Jewish penicillin comes as a bowl of clear broth filled with hunks of chicken and sprinkled with onions and cilantro. Regardless of your ills, it's a universal elixir. Restaurant owner Leon Singer is also an actor with lots of movie, TV, and stage credits. Photos of Singer and his friends in the act fill the restaurant lobby.

Honors & awards: Silver Medallion Awards, California Critics Awards.

Emerald Chinese Restaurant

Chinese Seafood

★★★

Inexpensive / Moderate

Quality 88   Value C

Zone 4   Mission Valley and the Mesas
3709 Convoy Street
565-6888

Reservations:	Recommended
When to go:	Any time
Entree range:	$8–18
Payment:	VISA, MC, AMEX, DC
Service rating:	★★
Friendliness rating:	★
Parking:	Free lot, street
Bar:	Limited
Wine selection:	House
Dress:	Dressy casual, informal
Disabled access:	Yes
Customers:	Locals, businesspeople, ethnic
Lunch:	Every day, 11 A.M.–3 P.M.
Dinner:	Every day, 5 P.M.–midnight

Atmosphere / setting: Though it's a shopping center location, the restaurant approaches elegance with its nice carpeting, tablecloths, and soothing emerald, brass, and grey color scheme. The room on the far left is the most quiet, but if you're going for dim sum, it's the last stop on the cart route.

House specialties: Live seafood.

Other recommendations: Dim sum—barbecued shrimp, pork, and scallions; turnip cakes; fried squid; black bean spare ribs; fresh custard.

Summary & comments: Home to almost 60 different types of delicious and sometimes outstanding dim sum, the Emerald features both the familiar and the eccentric. In the evening, only the standard menu is available, and there are some terrific options. Seafood is a house specialty, as you will quickly see from all the tanks with live creatures.

EMPEROR's PALACE

Zone 1   North County Inland
11835 Carmel Mountain Road
673-2279

Chinese / Mandarin & Szechuan
★★★
Inexpensive

Quality 80   Value B

Reservations:	Accepted
When to go:	Dinner
Entree range:	$6–17
Payment:	VISA, MC, AMEX
Service rating:	★★★
Friendliness rating:	★★
Parking:	Free lot
Bar:	Limited
Wine selection:	House
Dress:	Informal
Disabled access:	Yes
Customers:	Locals
Open:	Sunday–Thursday, 10:30 A.M.–9:30 P.M.;
	Friday and Saturday, 10:30 A.M.–10 P.M.

Atmosphere / setting: Mostly it looks like a large new suburban Chinese restaurant with tablecloths and silk plants. Inexplicably, there are also two big-screen TVs that are most often tuned to sporting events, but the sound is turned off.

House specialties: Pan-fried soft noodles; baby bok choy in garlic sauce; hot and sour eggplant; vegetable moo shi; sizzling rice soup Shanghai; kung pao beef.

Other recommendations: Dry braised shrimp in hot and sour sauce; shredded pork chungking; braised bean sprouts; beef with tomatoes.

Summary & comments: Only the house specials are truly outstanding; otherwise the fare is rather ordinary. The house soft noodles are especially good and a great bargain since they include beef, chicken, and shrimp. If your server is willing to engage in conversation, ask for dishes off the Chinese menu—which isn't really a menu, but reflects instead any special ingredients the kitchen got hold of that day.

EPAZOTE

Zone 2   North County Coastal
Del Mar Plaza,
   1555 Camino Del Mar, Del Mar
259-9966

Southwestern

★ ★ ★

Inexpensive / Moderate

Quality 85   Value C

Reservations:	Recommended
When to go:	Any time
Entree range:	$8–19
Payment:	VISA, MC, AMEX
Service rating:	★ ★
Friendliness rating:	★ ★
Parking:	Fee lot, valet
Bar:	Full service
Wine selection:	Extensive
Dress:	Dressy casual
Disabled access:	Yes
Customers:	Locals, businesspeople, visitors / tourists
Brunch:	Sunday, 10 A.M.–5 P.M.
Lunch:	Monday–Saturday, 11:30 A.M.–5 P.M.
Dinner:	Every day, 5 P.M.–midnight

Atmosphere / setting: It's somewhere between Southwestern Resort and Mexican Resort, but "resort" is the operative word. There's color, light, excitement, and a large outdoor seating area with a dreamy ocean view.

House specialties: Roasted garlic plate; green corn tamale; crab and chile corn cakes; spicy meat loaf club on Navajo flatbread; barbecued quail; smoked chicken relleno; barbecued tuna tostada.

Other recommendations: Charbroiled vegetable salad; three cheese and corn chile relleno; lamb chops with wild mushrooms; spit-roasted chicken.

Entertainment & amenities: Live blues on Tuesdays, jazz on Wednesdays.

Summary & comments: Friday night is like walking into a tornado of pulsing music, cascading hair, significant eye contact, and a hungry bunch of young professionals on the prowl. Getting to your table might mean threading through a bar scene like you were body surfing the Pacific. Once seated though, you'll see that the Santa Fe menu has diversity and genuine appeal, though your best bet will be to stick with the simpler dishes. The more things get exotic, the greater the risk of something going wrong. The noise level tends to be pretty high unless you're on the patio, but there's so much to look at, you probably won't be doing much talking anyway. It's a lot less gamy the rest of the week.

Honors & awards: Gold Award, Southern California Restaurant Writers Association.

Extraordinary Desserts

Zone 6   Downtown/Uptown/Central
2829 Fifth Avenue
294-7001

<table>
<tr><td>Desserts/Coffee</td></tr>
<tr><td>★★★</td></tr>
<tr><td>Inexpensive</td></tr>
<tr><td>Quality 85   Value D</td></tr>
</table>

Reservations:	Not accepted except for large private functions
When to go:	After theater, after a concert, or after a fat-free dinner
Entree range:	$4–7
Payment:	VISA, MC
Service rating:	★
Friendliness rating:	★
Parking:	Free lot, street
Bar:	None
Wine selection:	Not available
Dress:	Informal
Disabled access:	Yes
Customers:	Locals, visitors/tourists
Open:	Monday–Thursday, 8:30 A.M.–11 P.M.; Friday, 8:30 A.M.–midnight; Saturday, 11 A.M.–midnight; Sunday, 2–11 P.M.

Atmosphere/setting: It's a tiny and sophisticated cottage that effectively marries a coffee-house function with the charm of a wonderful stage set. You stand in line to order, then desserts and coffees are brought to your table.

House specialties: Chocolate gianduja crème brûlée; caramel macadamia cheesecake; cherry chocolate chip cookies; passion fruit napoleons; kona coffee nougat ice cream.

Other recommendations: Moroccan chocolate cake; coconut macaroons; lemon ricotta torte; chocolate mousse torte; lemon praline.

Entertainment & amenities: Enclosed garden patio.

Summary & comments: Karen Krasne is a local entrepreneur whose extraordinary baking skills are fully matched by her striking designer's eye. Desserts are wrapped in ribbons, festooned with flowers, flecked with gold, spun with sugar, and laid on with the grace and surge of a classical ballet. The crowd is as diverse in dress, age, and income as you'll find anywhere on the planet, but everyone has at least one thing in common: a love of sugar, cream, and chocolate.

Honors & awards: Best Desserts, *San Diego Magazine* 1992, 1993, 1994.

Fifth & Hawthorn

Zone 6   Downtown/Uptown/Central
515 Hawthorn Street
544-0940

California/Pacific Rim
★★
Moderate

Quality 79   Value C

Reservations:	Recommended
When to go:	Any time
Entree range:	$12–20
Payment:	VISA, MC, AMEX
Service rating:	★★
Friendliness rating:	★★★
Parking:	Street
Bar:	Full service
Wine selection:	Good
Dress:	Dressy casual
Disabled access:	Yes, but not to bathrooms
Customers:	Locals, businesspeople
Lunch:	Monday–Friday, 11:30 A.M.–2:30 P.M.;
	Saturday and Sunday, closed.
Dinner:	Sunday–Thursday, 5–9:30 P.M.;
	Friday and Saturday, 5–10:30 P.M.

Atmosphere/setting: Though it seems like a house that's been converted to a restaurant, it's more likely an office that's gone through the transformation. There are a few booths, but mostly there are small tables crisply set against a background of grey carpeting and walls. Decorations are few, but the setting is intimate.

House specialties: New dinner menu printed daily; it typically includes catfish, scallops, salmon, sea bass, ahi, rock shrimp, and calamari, and occasionally escolar and soft-shell crabs.

Other recommendations: Chicken breast; filet mignon; filet and scampi combo.

Summary & comments: It probably ought to be tucked into a quiet residential area. Instead, this smart and cordial neighborhood restaurant is actually located in an environ made up almost exclusively of small offices. To be here feels like you share in one of the secrets of San Diego since only the knowing would lead you to Fifth & Hawthorn. At lunchtime, the crowd is mostly made up of businesspeople; in the evening it's mostly couples.

Honors & awards: *San Diego Magazine,* First Place in Service/Moderate Price; last six of seven years—California Restaurant Writers Association, Gold Star Awards.

Filippi's Pizza Grotto

	Italian / Pizza
	★★
	Inexpensive
	Quality 75 Value B

Zone 1   North County Inland
114 West Grand, Escondido
747-2650

Zone 6   Downtown/Uptown/Central
1747 India Street
232-5095

Zone 8   Coronado/South Bay/Tijuana
82 Broadway, Chula Vista
422-9674

Reservations:	Accepted
When to go:	Evenings
Entree range:	$5–13
Payment:	VISA, MC, AMEX, DC, D
Service rating:	★★
Friendliness rating:	★★
Parking:	Free lot, street
Bar:	Limited
Wine selection:	House
Dress:	Informal
Disabled access:	No
Customers:	Locals, businesspeople, visitors/tourists
Open:	Every day, 11 A.M.–closing hours vary with each location and day of week; call the particular location for specific information.

Atmosphere/setting: At the India Street location, you must walk through an Italian grocery store to get to the restaurant. Once in the back, a new room opens and suddenly the lighting is low, plastic grapes dangle from the ceiling, and the tables are covered with checkered cloths. It looks like a Hollywood set for an old-fashioned pizzeria. Most other locations are straightforward pizza parlors.

House specialties: Cheese pizza; eight-item pizzas; lasagna with sausage and meatballs.

Other recommendations: Pepper steak sandwich; antipasto salad.

Summary & comments: In the heart of San Diego's Little Italy, Filippi's is a pizza parlor that's both old world and exotic. There are couples, families, noise, hustling waitresses, a limited menu, cheap table wine, and large gooey wheels of pizza. It's neither chic nor the finest pizza in town, but it is bustling, authentic, and convivial; they simply don't come this way anymore. There are Filippi's in many parts of San Diego, but India Street is the original and still the most interesting.

FINS

Zone 1   North County Inland
15817 Bernardo Center Drive, Suite 104
484-FINS

Zone 3   La Jolla
8657 Villa La Jolla Drive, #103, La Jolla
270-FINS

Zone 4   Mission Valley and the Mesas
9460H Mira Mesa Boulevard
549-FINS

Zone 4   Mission Valley and the Mesas
1640 Camino Del Rio North, Mission Valley Center
283-FINS

Baja-Style Mexican	
★★★	
Inexpensive	
Quality 89	Value B

Reservations:	Not accepted
When to go:	Any time
Entree range:	$2–5
Payment:	Cash only
Service rating:	★★
Friendliness rating:	★★★
Parking:	Free lot
Bar:	Beer is available at the Mira Mesa location only
Wine selection:	None
Dress:	Informal
Disabled access:	Yes
Customers:	Locals
Open:	Monday–Saturday, 10 A.M.–9 P.M.; Sunday, 11 A.M.–9 P.M. (Bernardo Center); every day, 10 A.M.–10 P.M. (La Jolla and Mira Mesa)

Atmosphere / setting: A fast-food environment with a playful and fishy theme.

House specialties: Shrimp burritos so perfect that seduction is instant.

Other recommendations: Shrimp and fish tacos; carne asada, chicken, carnitas burritos; chicken taquitos; coral reef mud pies.

Entertainment & amenities: Eclectic CD music mix, different every day and at all locations.

Summary & comments: A Surf's Up version of Mexican food where everything is crisp and bright and easy to manage. There's much to choose from on the menu, but the absolute best of everything is wrapped up in a chubby shrimp burrito. Other familiar items are available too, but if you order them you miss the point.

114

Fio's

Zone 6   Downtown/Uptown/Central
801 Fifth Avenue
234-3467

★★★
Moderate

Quality 89   Value C

Reservations:	Recommended
When to go:	Any time
Entree range:	$7–22
Payment:	VISA, MC, AMEX, DC, D
Service rating:	★★
Friendliness rating:	★★
Parking:	Valet, street
Bar:	Full service
Wine selection:	Extensive
Dress:	Dressy casual
Disabled access:	Yes
Customers:	Locals, businesspeople, visitors/tourists
Lunch:	Monday–Friday, 11:30 A.M.–3 P.M.; Saturday and Sunday, closed.
Dinner:	Monday–Thursday, 5–11 P.M.; Friday and Saturday, 5 P.M.–midnight; Sunday, 5–10 P.M.

Atmosphere/setting: Just a block from Horton Plaza, Fio's large street-level windows give approaching diners and passersby a preview of a smart-set restaurant. Inside is a huge vase of flowers, lots of small cloth-covered tables, music occasionally provided by a baby grand player piano, and wall alcoves filled with colossal canvases of ancient Sienna horse races.

House specialties: Soft polenta with mozzarella and wild mushrooms; salmon stuffed with fennel, onion, and dill; pollo alla fiorentina; shrimp, clams, scallops, and mussels in a spicy tomato broth; osso buco; grilled rabbit with rosemary.

Other recommendations: Pizza with grilled vegetables; roasted chicken with lemon and basil; pappardelle with shrimp and broccoli; lobster ravioli.

Summary & comments: Though San Diego's Gaslamp area is a hopping place now, it wasn't always so. At the turning point, Fio's was the first restaurant to bring sophisticated diners downtown after dark. The menu is a rambling mix of old and new and Northern and Southern Italian. There's a bistro-like frankness to the food that's usually congenial and now and again exceptional. Pastas are available in full and half portions and pizzas are made in a wood-fired oven.

Honors & awards: Five Gold Medallion Awards, San Diego Restaurant Association; *Wine Spectator* Award of Excellence; *San Diego Magazine* Readers' Poll, Best Italian.

The Fish Market/ Top of the Market

	Seafood
	★★★
	Moderate/Expensive

Zone 2   North County Coastal
640 Via de la Valle, Del Mar
755-2277

| Quality 89 | Value C |

Zone 6   Downtown/Uptown/Central
750 North Harbor Drive
232-3474

Reservations:	Only for 8 or more downstairs; recommended upstairs
When to go:	Any time
Entree range:	$7–30
Payment:	VISA, MC, AMEX, DC, D
Service rating:	★★★
Friendliness rating:	★★
Parking:	Fee lot during the day, meters (Del Mar); free lot and valet at night (Harbor Drive)
Bar:	Full service
Wine selection:	Extensive
Dress:	Dressy casual, informal; business attire, dressy casual upstairs (Harbor Drive)
Disabled access:	Yes
Customers:	Locals, businesspeople, visitors/tourists
Lunch/Dinner:	Every day, 11 A.M.–10 P.M.
Brunch:	Sunday, 10 A.M.–2 P.M. (Harbor Drive only)

Atmosphere/setting: Fish Markets are large and bustling, like immense and informal chowder houses. The Top of the Market is upstairs at the Harbor Drive location only. Though the room is very large, there is carpeting and tablecloths and a much greater sense of elegance. Even the same bay view seems more lavish.

House specialties: Dungeness crab cioppino; garlic prawns; Catalina swordfish; house-smoked fish; sushi; grilled ahi.

Other recommendations: Scallops with bacon; soft-shell crab (in season); Hawaiian tombo; Alaskan halibut; chinook salmon; Maine lobster; Petrale sole; free-range chicken; rib-eye steak.

Summary & comments: There is lots of excellent fresh fish and seafood here, and the very broad choices range from traditional treatments to sushi, with a variety of oysters in between. Both locations are impossibly noisy, though the Del Mar restaurant is the louder of the two. The decibel level gets halved at Top of the Market, but the prices are higher.

French Gourmet

	California French
	★★★
	Inexpensive/Moderate
	Quality 80 Value C

Zone 3   La Jolla
711 Pearl Street
454-6736
Zone 5   Mission Bay and Beaches
960 Turquoise Street
488-1725

Reservations:	Recommended
When to go:	Any time
Entree range:	$8–14
Payment:	VISA, MC, AMEX, DC
Service rating:	★★
Friendliness rating:	★★
Parking:	Free lot, street
Bar:	Limited
Wine selection:	Good
Dress:	Dressy casual, informal
Disabled access:	Yes
Customers:	Locals, businesspeople
Breakfast:	Every day, 8 A.M.–2 P.M.
Lunch:	Every day, 11 A.M.–2 P.M.
Dinner:	Sunday–Thursday, 4–10 P.M.;
	Friday and Saturday, 4–11 P.M.

Atmosphere/setting: Small and showing its age, the Pearl Street restaurant has blue Naugahyde booths, white tile floors, and too many small glass-topped tables crowded into the center of the room. Seating is also available outside. The Turquoise Street restaurant is newer and more vibrant, though still working a tight space.

House specialties: Quiche; Sylvia's Salad; chicken pot pie; chicken Diablo; steamed mussels; braised medallions of lamb; veal sweetbreads; salmon tarte.

Other recommendations: Catfish Dijonnaise; duck with raspberries; veal piccata; petrale sole with capers.

Summary & comments: A casual, unpretentious bistro with a small menu, a long local history, and a dedicated following, the French Gourmet also does a thriving catering business and operates a bakery next door to the Pearl Street restaurant. It's also begun supplying the Price Club with breads and fancy pastries.

French Market Grill

	French
	★★
	Moderate
	Quality 78 Value D

Zone 1   North County Inland
15717 Bernardo Heights Parkway
485-8055

Reservations:	Accepted
When to go:	Any time
Entree range:	Lunch, $7–11; dinner, $16–18
Payment:	VISA, MC
Service rating:	★★
Friendliness rating:	★★★
Parking:	Free lot
Bar:	Limited
Wine selection:	Good
Dress:	Dressy casual
Disabled access:	Yes
Customers:	Locals
Open:	Sunday–Thursday, 8 A.M.–9 P.M.;
	Friday and Saturday, 8 A.M.–10 P.M.

Atmosphere / setting: There's a deli display case at the entrance, tile floors, a fireplace that's always lit, and a charming outdoor seating area. Daytime, the look is coffeehouse / bistro; nighttime, it's the same, only more dressed up.

House specialties: Onion soup; steamed clams marinière; smoked chicken quesadilla; escargot en baguette; lamb shanks on a white bean cassoulet; grilled Black Angus New York steak; trio of prawns with mushroom ravioli.

Other recommendations: Coq au vin; wild mushroom ravioli with chicken breast and spinach; spicy chicken pizza; cioppino Mediterranean; rotisseried chicken.

Summary & comments: Most recently a coffeehouse that served light meals, the French Market Grill has been converted into a bistro that also wants to be a dinner restaurant. Both the manager and chef are owners, and both are alums of one of the better hotel restaurants in town. Menu changes and price increases are frequent. Food tends toward the traditional, which is what most of the patrons in this suburban shopping center seem to be looking for.

Galaxy Grill

Zone 6 Downtown/Uptown/Central	American
522 Horton Plaza	★★
234-7211	Inexpensive
	Quality 76 Value B

Reservations:	Not accepted
When to go:	Lunch
Entree range:	$4–6
Payment:	VISA, MC, D
Service rating:	★★
Friendliness rating:	★★
Parking:	Free lot
Bar:	Limited
Wine selection:	House
Dress:	Informal
Disabled access:	Yes
Customers:	Locals, visitors/tourists
Open:	Monday–Thursday, 11 A.M.–9 P.M.;
	Friday and Saturday, 11 A.M.–10 P.M.;
	Sunday, 11 A.M.–8 P.M.

Atmosphere/setting: It's a TV version of a 1950s soda fountain, complete with a genuine (if small-scale) fountain, red leatherette stools, over-stuffed booths, chrome trim, and waitresses in bobby sox.

House specialties: Hamburgers; Philly cheese steak; meat loaf; ice cream sodas; malts; and shakes.

Other recommendations: Tuna salad; grilled cheese; tuna melt; BLT; onion rings.

Summary & comments: An ideal place to rest your dogs during a day of shopping at Horton Plaza, the Galaxy Grill is one of the few remaining stops for a grilled cheese sandwich or a tomato stuffed with tuna. The french fries are as tasty as they were in the '50s. Ditto for the chocolate shakes. As a concession to modern times, there's an excellent vegeburger available. Food is as straightforward as it was in the heyday of *Ladies Home Journal* and the *Saturday Evening Post,* and you'll get no surprises.

Gelato Vero Caffe

Zone 6   Downtown/Uptown/Central
3753 India Street
295-9269

Reservations:	Not accepted
When to go:	Any time
Entree range:	$2–4
Payment:	AMEX
Service rating:	★
Friendliness rating:	★
Parking:	Street
Bar:	None
Wine selection:	Not available
Dress:	Informal
Disabled access:	Yes
Customers:	Locals
Open:	Monday–Thursday, 6 A.M.–midnight;
	Friday, 6 A.M.–1 A.M.; Saturday, 7 A.M.–1 A.M.;
	Sunday, 7 A.M.–midnight

Atmosphere/setting: The inside is all isle, narrow as a phone booth, with a small back room set with a few tables and chairs and scattered newspapers. Outside on the cramped sidewalk, tables and chairs hug the building closely. It's all functional and in a bit of disarray.

House specialties: Homemade gelatos and sorbets; coffees and teas.

Other recommendations: Pastries; cakes; tarts.

Entertainment & amenities: Live music weekend evenings.

Summary & comments: From early morning to late at night, this is the pantheon of cool. If the service were any more laid back it might be nonexistent, but there's a palpable sense that anyone frustrated by the entrenched casualness and ennui is too uptight for words. The coffees and teas are very good and the gelato is wonderful. Also, the corner at which Gelato Vero sits (Washington and India streets) is a perfect place to spend an hour reading the paper and watching the passing scene. If you spend all morning there, you have only to move a few doors down the street to do lunch at Saffron.

Honors & awards: *San Diego Union,* Best Ice Cream; Warner Books, *The Very Best Ice Cream and Where to Find It.*

GEORGE'S CAFE
and OCEAN TERRACE

Zone 3   La Jolla
1250 Prospect Street
454-4244

American Bistro	
★★★	
Moderate	
Quality 84	Value C

Reservations:	Recommended
When to go:	Lunchtime or early evening, when you can see the water view
Entree range:	Lunch, $8–11; dinner, $8–15
Payment:	VISA, MC, AMEX, DC, D
Service rating:	★★★
Friendliness rating:	★★★
Parking:	Street, valet in the evening
Bar:	Full service
Wine selection:	Extensive
Dress:	Informal
Disabled access:	Yes
Customers:	Locals, businesspeople, visitors/tourists
Open:	Sunday–Thursday, 11 A.M.–10 P.M.; Friday and Saturday, 11 A.M.–11 P.M.

Atmosphere/setting: The Ocean Terrace is a flat slab roof with railings and very nice outdoor tables, chairs, and umbrellas. The breathtaking view is of a simple flat slab of blue ocean. One flight down is the Cafe, which feels like a bar with a wide open window that lets the view in. If you've been outside on the terrace, you might feel claustrophobic in the cafe.

House specialties: Fish tacos; smoked chicken and black bean soup; muscovy duck leg confit; Niçoise salad; swordfish with horseradish cream; thresher shark sandwich.

Other recommendations: Grilled pork chops; seafood sampler; grilled chicken breast salad; white sea bass with lemon juice and capers.

Summary & comments: The food is typically very good at George's, but it's the setting of the Ocean Terrace that gets the most raves. To sit out there, day or night, feels as if you're aboard ship. In addition to the view, the Ocean Terrace is exceptionally popular because you can get George's well-regarded food at a slightly lower price than at the formal indoor restaurant. Of course, though the kitchen is the same, the menu is different.

George's at the Cove

	California
Zone 3 La Jolla	★★★★
1250 Prospect Street	Moderate/Expensive
454-4244	Quality 92 Value C

Reservations:	Recommended
When to go:	Any time when you can see the ocean
Entree range:	Lunch, $8–15; dinner, $17–30
Payment:	VISA, MC, AMEX, DC, D
Service rating:	★★★
Friendliness rating:	★★★
Parking:	Valet in the evenings, street
Bar:	Full service
Wine selection:	Extensive
Dress:	Dressy casual
Disabled access:	Yes
Customers:	Locals, businesspeople, visitors/tourists
Lunch:	Every day, 11:30 A.M.–2:30 P.M.
Dinner:	Sunday–Thursday, 5:30–10 P.M.;
	Friday and Saturday, 5:30–11 P.M.

Atmosphere/setting: There are two principal dining areas. The main (front) room is poshly done with white wicker and boasts a glorious ocean view. The rear room feels woody and library-like, and though very pleasant, it lacks the style and comfort of up-front dining.

House specialties: Foie gras charred on mushrooms; sautéed whitefish with potato crust; rack of lamb with a Chinese mustard glaze; halibut in a chicken fumet; applewood-smoked salmon with fennel; scallops layered with spinach and potatoes.

Other recommendations: Mahimahi with sweet cayenne vinaigrette; steamed black mussels; marinated octopus with polenta; two-pound Maine lobster; grilled pork chop on a cabbage and apple tart.

Summary & comments: George's at the Cove may be the most popular restaurant in La Jolla. The chef is terrific, the setting is lovely, the service is friendly, and owner George Hauer is usually hovering around to make sure things operate smoothly. But popularity also means the kitchen is sometimes overwhelmed, and both food and service may suffer.

Honors & awards: Most Popular Restaurant, *1996 Zagat Guide;* Best of the Best, *San Diego Magazine;* Three Stars, *Mobil Travel Guide.*

Grant Grill

	Continental
	★★★
Zone 6 Downtown/Uptown/Central	Moderate/Expensive
U.S. Grant Hotel, 326 Broadway	
232-3121	Quality 85 Value C

Reservations:	Recommended
When to go:	Any time
Entree range:	Lunch, $8–11; dinner, $15–23
Payment:	VISA, MC, AMEX, DC, D
Service rating:	★★★
Friendliness rating:	★★
Parking:	Fee lot (validations), valet, street
Bar:	Full service
Wine selection:	Extensive
Dress:	Business attire
Disabled access:	Yes
Customers:	Locals, businesspeople, visitors/tourists
Brunch:	Saturday and Sunday, 11:30 A.M.–2 P.M.
Lunch:	Monday–Friday, 11:30 A.M.–2 P.M.
Dinner:	Sunday–Thursday, 5:30–10 P.M.;
	Friday and Saturday, 5:30–10:30 P.M.

Atmosphere/setting: Filled as it is with wine-red booths and dark wood paneling, the Grill feels formal, formidable, and very men's clubish.

House specialties: Lobster and shrimp strudel; Cobb salad; chilled venison roast; homemade lamb sausage; veal chop with caramelized shallots and Calvados sauce; shrimp and oyster gratinée; pork tenderloin with napa cabbage; rack of lamb with honey and ginger glaze.

Other recommendations: T-bone steak; New York steak; roasted boneless game hen; grilled salmon with warm tomato relish; Grant Grill burger.

Summary & comments: This is one of the few restaurants left that still exudes an old-fashioned sense of having arrived. The Grant Grill feels so cushy and secure, you could probably rule forever from a perch in the dining room. The formal menu has a white-gloved staff equal to the challenge. The lobster and shrimp strudel is glorious, though simple dishes are generally the best. Desserts are gorgeous.

Honors & awards: Gold Medallion, Best Hotel Restaurant, San Diego Restaurant Association; Four Diamond Award of Excellence, American Automobile Association; *Wine Spectator* Award of Excellence.

Harry's Cafe Gallery

	American
	★★
	Inexpensive
	Quality 75 Value C

Zone 3   La Jolla
7545 Girard Avenue
454-7381

Reservations:	Not accepted
When to go:	Breakfast
Entree range:	$1–7
Payment:	VISA, MC, AMEX, DC, D
Service rating:	★★
Friendliness rating:	★★★
Parking:	Free lot, street
Bar:	None
Wine selection:	None
Dress:	Informal
Disabled access:	Yes
Customers:	Locals, businesspeople
Breakfast/Lunch:	Every day, 5:30 A.M.–2:30 P.M.

Atmosphere/setting: A seasoned old coffee shop on the edge of La Jolla's fashionable commercial area.

House specialties: Oatmeal; muffins; Belgian waffles; banana pancakes; thick French toast; cappuccino.

Other recommendations: Hot turkey; salads; soups; burgers.

Entertainment & amenities: An art gallery of sorts on the wall; many of the paintings and lithos are for sale.

Summary & comments: Harry's is part of the tradition of Old La Jolla, when things were simple and chic was not something you'd want to be known for. It's been family-owned and -operated for almost 40 years.

Hernandez' Hideaway

	Mexican
	★★★
	Inexpensive / Moderate
	Quality 80 Value B

Zone 1   North County Inland
19320 Lake Drive, Escondido
746-1444

Reservations:	Recommended
When to go:	Dinner
Entree range:	$7–13
Payment:	VISA, MC, AMEX, DC, D
Service rating:	★★
Friendliness rating:	★★
Parking:	Free lot
Bar:	Full service
Wine selection:	House
Dress:	Informal
Disabled access:	Yes
Customers:	Locals
Brunch:	Saturday and Sunday, 10 A.M.–2 P.M.
Dinner:	Tuesday–Saturday, 3–9 P.M.;
	Sunday and Monday, closed.

Atmosphere / setting: Like a vestige from the '70s that feels like it's from the '50s, Hernandez' sits just a few feet above Lake Hodges and occupies a world entirely its own. There's a central bar and several seemingly disjointed, always-crowded rooms that radiate from it. Decor varies slightly in each room, but the organizing theme seems to involve paper flowers and bunkhouse references.

House specialties: Carnitas platter (roughly shredded hunks of roasted pork, beans and rice, guacamole, cilantro, and melted cheese); quesadillas; chile rellenos.

Other recommendations: Shrimp burrito; sour cream chicken enchiladas.

Summary & comments: Authenticity drips not just from the overwrought decor and the familiar Mexican menu, but also from the food that comes in such generous portions that it spills over the edges of plates. There's virtually no subtlety and nothing low fat here, but much of the food is lusty and satisfying. Hernandez' attracts lots of families, cowboys, and city folk young and old.

Hob Nob Hill

Zone 6   Downtown / Uptown / Central
2271 First Avenue
239-8176

American
★
Inexpensive / Moderate
Quality 75   Value B

Reservations:	Recommended
When to go:	Breakfast
Entree range:	$3–15
Payment:	VISA, MC, AMEX, D
Service rating:	★★★
Friendliness rating:	★★★
Parking:	Street
Bar:	None
Wine selection:	House
Dress:	Business attire, informal
Disabled access:	Yes
Customers:	Locals, businesspeople
Breakfast:	Every day, 7 A.M.–9 P.M.
Lunch:	Every day, 11 A.M.–4 P.M.
Dinner:	Every day, 4–9 P.M.

Atmosphere / setting: The look of it is of a dining room in a business hotel in the heyday of *Father Knows Best*. Wood-grained formica and red Naugahyde mix with chintz window trim and glass cases displaying huge slices of pies and cakes. There are two rooms here: one is all booths and the other is all tables. "Nothing fancy" describes it perfectly.

House specialties: Western omelets; cream of wheat; pancake sandwiches; liver with onions and eggs; roast beef hash; coffee cake; cinnamon rolls.

Other recommendations: Eggs Benedict; lamb shank; braised short ribs; turkey croquettes.

Summary & comments: What's extraordinary about this San Diego institution is that the location is just on the outskirts of convenience but there's always a crush at breakfast time. In the evening, the clientele shifts toward a preponderance of seniors. Food is of the homey variety, the sort that TV moms in the '50s lavished on the family. At breakfast, your poached eggs on toast come with canned apple filling on the side, and your jam arrives in hollowed-out oranges. Waitresses are older, efficient, and have names like Mable and Pearl. In the midst of this abundant quaintness, more breakfast meetings are held and more major deals sealed than probably any office in the entire region.

Honors & awards: *San Diego Union Tribune,* Best Breakfast, Best Family Dining.

Hops! Bistro & Brewery

<table>
<tr><td>American</td></tr>
<tr><td>★★★</td></tr>
<tr><td>Inexpensive</td></tr>
<tr><td>Quality 85   Value B</td></tr>
</table>

Zone 4   Mission Valley and the Mesas
University Towne Center,
   4353 La Jolla Village Drive
587-6677

Zone 6   Downtown/Uptown/Central
310 Fifth Avenue
232-6336

Reservations:	Recommended
When to go:	Any time
Entree range:	$7–10
Payment:	VISA, MC, AMEX, DC, D
Service rating:	★★
Friendliness rating:	★★
Parking:	Free lot
Bar:	Full service
Wine selection:	Extensive
Dress:	Informal
Disabled access:	Yes
Customers:	Locals, visitors/tourists
Open:	Monday–Thursday, 11 A.M.–10 P.M.;
	Friday and Saturday, 11 A.M.–10:30 P.M.;
	Sunday, 10 A.M.–9 P.M.

Atmosphere/setting: A beer hall for the '90s, with lots of tables, glass windows, and shiny wall decor. Upbeat tempo.

House specialties: Grilled chicken and garlic mashed potatoes; charbroiled fish; sauced-up pastas; microbrewed beer.

Other recommendations: Blackened shrimp salad; grilled mahimahi; pork chops; grilled steak sandwich with mozzarella.

Summary & comments: This is a conspicuously hip microbrewery and restaurant in the University Towne Center shopping mall. Particularly at night, Hops! feels a bit like being inside a Wurlitzer. There's so much sound and light that it's all a little dizzying. The signature dish is the rather ordinary sounding grilled chicken with garlic mashed potatoes. Also, order a taster set of the beers to figure out which you like the most and to get a sense of the diversity available.

Humphrey's

	Seafood
	★★
	Moderate / Expensive
	Quality 72 Value C

Zone 5   Mission Bay and Beaches
2241 Shelter Island Drive
224-3577

Reservations:	Recommended
When to go:	Sunday brunch
Entree range:	Lunch, $6–10; dinner, $16–37
Payment:	VISA, MC, AMEX, DC, D
Service rating:	★★
Friendliness rating:	★★
Parking:	Free if you can find a parking space, otherwise you'll have to use a fee lot
Bar:	Full service
Wine selection:	Good
Dress:	Dressy casual, informal
Disabled access:	Yes
Customers:	Locals, visitors / tourists
Breakfast:	Monday–Saturday, 7–11 A.M.; Sunday, 7–9:30 A.M.
Brunch:	Sunday, 10–2 P.M.
Lunch:	Monday–Friday, 11 A.M.–2 P.M.; Saturday, 11 A.M.–3 P.M.
Dinner:	Sunday–Thursday, 5:30–10 P.M.; Friday and Saturday, 5:30–11 P.M.

Atmosphere / setting: It's big and old, but has a great marina view.

House specialties: Clam bake (two-pound Maine lobster with cockles, mussels, and corn on the cob); Hawaiian spearfish; halibut tostada; Cajun burger.

Other recommendations: Filet mignon; grilled shrimp and scallops; fresh oysters.

Entertainment & amenities: Lounge entertainment seven nights a week. During the summer, Humphrey's hosts a four-month concert series featuring some of the best music and comedic performers in the country.

Summary & comments: It's the Sunday brunch, which is lavish, the water view, which is lush, and the concert series, which is filled with show stoppers, that keeps Humphrey's going strong.

IchibAN

Zone 5   Mission Bay and Beaches
1441 Garnet
270-5755

Zone 6   Downtown/Uptown/Central
1449 University Avenue
299-7203

Japanese	
★★★	
Inexpensive	
Quality 80	Value A

Reservations:	Not accepted
When to go:	Any time
Entree range:	$5–8
Payment:	Cash only
Service rating:	★★
Friendliness rating:	★
Parking:	Street
Bar:	None
Wine selection:	None
Dress:	Informal
Disabled access:	Yes
Customers:	Locals
Lunch:	Every day, 11:30 A.M.–2:30 P.M. (Garnet)
Dinner:	Every day, 5–9:30 P.M. (Garnet)
Open:	Every day, 11:30 A.M.–9:30 P.M. (University)

Atmosphere/setting: Once it may have been the butcher's or the baker's shop on University Avenue. Now it's just a small store with deli cases, a few closely spaced tables, giveaway newspapers, flyers about local events, and a community bulletin board. The greater number of tables and chairs are out on the sidewalk.

House specialties: Mixed sashimi; California maki; teriyaki chicken; garlic seafood; fried vegetables; stamina noodles.

Other recommendations: Gyoza; shumai; miso; curry bowl; seafood soup with vegetables.

Summary & comments: Wildly popular, Ichiban is the place for good-tasting, inexpensive Japanese food. There's a line at the counter where you order and pay, and they'll bring your meal to you when it's ready. Though probably not the first place you'll want to head if you're hankering exotic food, it's an excellent choice for traditional sushi, soups, noodles, tempura, and Bento boxes. The crowd consists of lots of students, the budget-minded, and sentimentalists yearning for the camaraderie of the '60s.

Il Fornaio Cucina Italiana / Enoteca Fornaio

	Italian
	★★
	Moderate
	Quality 79 Value C

Zone 2   North County Coastal
Del Mar Plaza,
   1555 Camino del Mar, Del Mar
755-8876

Reservations:	Recommended
When to go:	Any time
Entree range:	$7–17
Payment:	VISA, MC, AMEX, DC
Service rating:	★★
Friendliness rating:	★★
Parking:	Free lot, valet
Bar:	Full service
Wine selection:	Extensive
Dress:	Dressy casual
Disabled access:	Yes
Customers:	Locals, businesspeople, visitors / tourists
Brunch:	Sunday, 10 A.M.–3 P.M.
Lunch:	Every day, 11:30 A.M.–5 P.M.
Dinner:	Sunday–Thursday, 5–11 P.M.;
	Friday and Saturday, 5 P.M.–midnight

Atmosphere / setting: Located in Del Mar Plaza, which itself is modeled on an Italian hill town, Il Fornaio exudes the air of a stylish Italian bistro. There's an open kitchen, gleaming copper, lots of imported marble, and sleek tables and chairs. The outside patio is glorious on most days.

House specialties: Pasta filled with lobster and leeks; grilled veal chop with sage and rosemary; veal scaloppine with fresh artichokes; grilled duck; rabbit wrapped in pancetta; eggplant and smoked mozzarella pizza.

Other recommendations: Fresh tomato soup with Tuscan bread; grilled polenta with provolone, mushrooms, and truffle oil; pan-roasted chicken breast; duck lasagna; fresh vegetable soup.

Summary & comments: It tends to be a little noisy and hectic, and the cooking isn't uniform, but Il Fornaio is still an extraordinarily popular place that's in the thick of whatever is happening. What's more, the restaurant helps support the Enoteca, which sits immediately across the plaza. The Enoteca Fornaio offers one of the most extensive libraries of Italian wine in the county. It's a wonderful place to be any time it's open. Plenty of locals who think San Diego is the end of the rainbow think the Enoteca is where the pot of gold is.

Indigo Grill

Zone 6   Downtown / Uptown / Central
1702 India Street
234-5456

Southwestern
★★★★
Inexpensive / Moderate

Quality 90   Value A

Reservations:	Recommended
When to go:	Lunch or dinner
Entree range:	$9–23
Payment:	VISA, MC, AMEX, DC, D
Service rating:	★★
Friendliness rating:	★★★
Parking:	Street
Bar:	Limited
Wine selection:	Good
Dress:	Dressy casual, informal
Disabled access:	Yes
Customers:	Locals, businesspeople, visitors / tourists
Breakfast:	Every day, 8–10:30 A.M.
Brunch:	Saturday, 8 A.M.–3 P.M.
Lunch:	Monday–Friday, 11 A.M.–3 P.M.; Sunday and Monday, closed.
Dinner:	Tuesday–Sunday, 4–10 P.M.; Monday, closed.

Atmosphere / setting: Located on the ground floor of a small hotel favored by budget-minded Europeans, the restaurant is a narrow **L**-shaped space nicely decorated in an informal southwestern style. A bank of windows rim one side of the restaurant and look out on the street.

House specialties: Butternut squash soup with pumpkin-seed pesto; warmed Brie with tomatillo sauce; warm caponata salad with farmer's cheese on onion-rosemary bread; beet ravioli stack; nut-crusted buffalo burger; cheese and chicken tamale.

Other recommendations: Barbecued chicken burrito with smoky black beans; pecan-crusted rainbow trout; snapper in parchment; ancho- and sage-rubbed T-bone steak; rabbit quesadillas.

Summary & comments: The big surprise here is the lavish imagination and the frequent chile-inspired heat. Most dishes come with both. When you order something like the beet ravioli, you get a wonderfully decorated plate bearing a strong resemblance to an ancient Yucatán-stepped pyramid; it's clearly based on the theme of ravioli rather than the stuffed Italian pasta. Along with the heat are frequent sweet spicings—cinnamon is a constant presence—and every dish seems to garner a "wow" response. Given the quality of the meal and the moderate pricing, it's a considerable value.

Islands

Zone 1   North County Inland
240 South Melrose Drive, Vista
631-1535

Zone 1   North County Inland
12224 Carmel Mountain Road
485-8075

Zone 4   Mission Valley and the Mesas
8657 Villa La Jolla Drive
455-9945

Reservations:	Not accepted
When to go:	Any time
Entree range:	$5–7
Payment:	VISA, MC, AMEX
Service rating:	★★★
Friendliness rating:	★★★★
Parking:	Free lot
Bar:	Limited
Wine selection:	House
Dress:	Informal
Disabled access:	Yes
Customers:	Locals, businesspeople
Lunch/Dinner:	Sunday–Thursday, 11:30 A.M.–9:30 P.M.;
	Friday and Saturday, 11 A.M.–10:30 P.M.

Atmosphere/setting: Hawaii, as seen in a surfer dude's dream, is a big place filled with plants, music, and happy people. That's Islands.

House specialties: Burgers; BLTs; Island fries; chicken fajitas.

Other recommendations: Spicy chicken salad; tuna salad; vegetarian taco.

Summary & comments: Child of the Chart House group, Islands is a chain of concept restaurants that push a laid-back Hawaiian theme with bright colors, lush plants, and some of the perkiest servers south of Disneyland. To its credit though, the exhilarated staff in shorts and Hawaiian shirts also serve terrific half-pound hamburgers in a variety of guises (barbecue sauce, guacamole, Swiss cheese, mushrooms, etc.) and undeniably fabulous french fries that come in a portion suitable for three. Pretty darn good are the soft tacos (warm flour tortillas) that wrap around a chicken fajita filling.

JAKE'S DEL MAR

Zone 2 North County Coastal	American
1660 Coast Boulevard, Del Mar	★★
755-2002	Moderate
Zone 8 Coronado /	Quality 75 Value C
South Bay / Tijuana	
530 Marina Boulevard, Chula Vista	
476-0400	

Reservations:	Recommended
When to go:	Evenings, especially in the summer
Entree range:	$7–20
Payment:	VISA, MC, AMEX
Service rating:	★★
Friendliness rating:	★★
Parking:	Free lot, valet, street
Bar:	Full service
Wine selection:	Good
Dress:	Dressy casual
Disabled access:	Yes
Customers:	Locals, visitors / tourists
Brunch:	Sunday, 10 A.M.–2:30 P.M.
Lunch:	Tuesday–Saturday, 11:15 A.M.–2:30 P.M.; Monday, closed.
Dinner:	Sunday–Thursday, 5–9:30 P.M.; Friday and Saturday, 5–10 P.M.

Atmosphere / setting: The original Del Mar location is spacious and woody, with several rooms, several levels, lots of tables and booths, and a persistent hip and upbeat quality. One room looks out over—and seems to be almost on—a sandy beach.

House specialties: Fresh fish specials; lobster; rack of lamb.

Other recommendations: Poached salmon; grilled calamari sandwich; ahi sashimi; seafood pasta Provençal.

Entertainment & amenities: Dining on the beach.

Summary & comments: Jake's is at the heart of the Southern California myth of beaches and blondness and days in the sun. If "Baywatch" were filmed in San Diego, Jake's is where the cast would undoubtedly hang out—and it's also where they'd bring their parents, aunts, and cousins. If you can make it for lunch or dinner when it's still light outside, try for a table that overlooks the beach.

Honors & awards: *San Diego Magazine* 1994, Best of the Best, Best Outdoor Dining, Best Burger, Best Value.

133

JASMINE

<table>
<tr><td>Zone 4</td><td>Mission Valley and the Mesas</td></tr>
</table>

4609 Convoy Street, Suite A
268-0888

Chinese
★★★★
Moderate

Quality 92   Value C

Reservations:	Accepted
When to go:	Any time
Entree range:	$6–25
Payment:	VISA, MC, AMEX
Service rating:	★★
Friendliness rating:	★
Parking:	Free lot
Bar:	Full service
Wine selection:	House
Dress:	Dressy casual
Disabled access:	Yes
Customers:	Locals, ethnic
Open:	Monday–Friday, 10 A.M.–midnight;
	Saturday and Sunday, 9:30 A.M.–midnight

Atmosphere / setting: It's large—almost aerodrome-sized—with lots of tables and lots of bustle. Grey carpeting, grey walls, and white tablecloths everywhere give it a slightly formal demeanor.

House specialties: Dim sum; barbecue platters (chicken, duck, spareribs, pork); braised shark fin; sizzling beef; diced chicken with hot pepper and bamboo shoots; steamed lobster with ginger and lemon; salted pork chop; assorted seafood pan-fried noodles.

Other recommendations: Roast pork lo mein; sautéed rock cod; crab or clams in black bean sauce; Singapore mai fun; eggplant with garlic sauce.

Summary & comments: Probably the best Chinese food in town is at Jasmine. The restaurant has an extraordinarily broad menu and a cadre of servers as numerous as an Idaho militia unit. At lunchtime and on weekends, the variety of dim sum is astounding and includes rock cod fish balls and pan-fried chive cakes along with more than 50 standard dishes. You can also order from the regular menu any time. The black bean crab, sizzling beef, and just about everything else is wonderful. Unfortunately, service is often confused and the restaurant is frequently booked for Chinese weddings and other celebrations, and only a few tables are set aside for drop-in diners.

Julian Pie Co.

<table>
<tr><td rowspan="4"></td><td>Desserts</td></tr>
<tr><td>★★</td></tr>
<tr><td>Inexpensive</td></tr>
<tr><td>Quality 77   Value B</td></tr>
</table>

Zone 1   North County Inland
2225 Main Street, Julian
765-2449

Zone 1   North County Inland
21976 Highway 79, Santa Ysabel
765-2400

Reservations:	Not accepted
When to go:	Any time
Entree range:	$2–8
Payment:	VISA, MC, AMEX, D
Service rating:	★★★
Friendliness rating:	★★★
Parking:	Street
Bar:	None
Wine selection:	None
Dress:	Informal
Disabled access:	Yes
Customers:	Visitors/tourists
Open:	Every day, 9 A.M.–5 P.M.

Atmosphere/setting: It's a little wooden house on Julian's only main street.

House specialties: Apple pies, some made with a variety of berries.

Entertainment & amenities: Sunday afternoon singing and playing on the front porch.

Summary & comments: Despite the fact that its soul is pledged to tourism, the small mountain town of Julian manages to retain a dribble or so of its original charm. And though people speak of the fine apple pies available there, really good pie will remain as elusive as a Sasquatch until you hit the Julian Pie Company. The bakery occupies a little house on the end of town where there is a permanent line of customers snaking out the front door. The apple pie here is as good as it gets, all moist and chunky with the warming smell of cinnamon and an ever-crispy, flaky crust. Incredibly, the pie even stands up to reheating in a microwave. The Julian Pie Company is one of the best reasons for visiting Julian.

Karinya Thai Cuisine

Zone 5 Mission Bay and the Beaches	Thai
4475 Mission Boulevard	★★★
270-5050	Inexpensive
	Quality 82 Value C

Reservations:	Accepted
When to go:	Dinner
Entree range:	$6–13
Payment:	VISA, MC
Service rating:	★
Friendliness rating:	★★
Parking:	Free lot
Bar:	Limited
Wine selection:	House
Dress:	Dressy casual, informal
Disabled access:	Yes
Customers:	Locals
Lunch:	Tuesday–Friday, 11:30 A.M.–2:30 P.M.; Saturday–Monday, closed.
Dinner:	Every day, 5:30–10 P.M.

Atmosphere / setting: Even with tapestries, sculpture, and fresh flowers, Karinya manages to create a low-key environment. There are three separate dining rooms, and though the room to the right of the front door seems a little nicer, it's only marginally so. There are only tables—no booths—and pink and celedon make up the basic color scheme.

House specialties: Stuffed chicken wings; spicy fish cakes with cucumber sauce; crispy fried whole fish; volcano chicken; fried lobster in shrimp sauce; scallops in red chile–paste curry.

Other recommendations: Chicken with oyster sauce; tofu with ginger sauce; barbecued chicken; minced beef sautéed with mint; duck with garlic and pepper marinade; beef in coconut milk curry.

Summary & comments: Karinya has one of the more pleasant Thai environments, but it looks better at night than during the day. The 70-item menu is filled with distinctively flavored and carefully seasoned food, so one dish rarely tastes like another. Do pay attention to the heat scale here because they truly listen. If you ask for a dish "medium-plus," you'd better mean it.

Honors & awards: Gold Award from Southern California Restaurant Writers Association, four years in a row.

Karl Strauss' Old Columbia Brewery & Grill

German/American
★★★
Inexpensive
Quality 80   Value B

Zone 3   La Jolla
1044 Wall Street
551-2739

Zone 4   Mission Valley and the Mesas
9675 Scranton Road
587-2739

Zone 6   Downtown/Uptown/Central
1157 Columbia Street
234-2739

Reservations:	Recommended
When to go:	Any time, but happy hours are especially convivial
Entree range:	$7–13
Payment:	VISA, MC
Service rating:	★★
Friendliness rating:	★★
Parking:	Street; free lot (Scranton Road)
Bar:	Limited
Wine selection:	House
Dress:	Informal
Disabled access:	Yes
Customers:	Locals, businesspeople
Lunch:	Every day, 11:30 A.M.–4:30 P.M.
Dinner:	Sunday–Wednesday, 4:30–10 P.M.; Thursday–Saturday, 4:30 P.M.–1 A.M.

Atmosphere/setting: The Columbia Street building is an old brick one remodeled for the restaurant. It has less the look of a beer hall than of a fern bar without the ferns. The Scranton Road location is a gigantic beer hall.

House specialties: Johnsonville sausages; beer-battered fish and chips; barbecued ribs.

Summary & comments: This was the first combination microbrewery and restaurant in town and it's been going strong for years. Homebrewed beers are excellent and there's a surprising amount of attention paid to the hefty salads, sausages, and grills. It's a very affable place for lunch or an after-work drink. One of the nicest features are the tasters—bargain-priced four-ounce samplers offering a few long sips of what's on tap. While the beer is the same at all locations, the food gets the most attention at Columbia.

Khyber Pass

<table>
<tr><td>Zone 4   Mission Valley and the Mesas</td><td>Afghani
★ ★ ★
Inexpensive / Moderate

Quality 82   Value C</td></tr>
</table>

Zone 4   Mission Valley and the Mesas
4647 Convoy Street
571-3749

Reservations:	Accepted
When to go:	Dinner
Entree range:	$7–13
Payment:	VISA, MC, AMEX, D
Service rating:	★ ★
Friendliness rating:	★ ★ ★
Parking:	Free lot
Bar:	Limited
Wine selection:	House
Dress:	Dressy casual
Disabled access:	Yes
Customers:	Locals, businesspeople
Lunch:	Monday–Saturday, 11 A.M.–2:30 P.M.; Sunday, closed.
Dinner:	Monday–Saturday, 5–10 P.M.; Sunday, closed.

Atmosphere / setting: Tucked into the back of a shopping center, Khyber Pass has a molded interior that drips (albeit in plaster) with the contours of a cave somewhere in Afghanistan. Brightly colored fabrics adorn the room, and every chair has a sash with bells.

House specialties: Aushak (scallion-filled dumplings); bulaunee (leek and potato turnover); bauraunee-baunjaun (sautéed eggplant with yogurt); beef sambosa; bauraunee-kadu (sautéed banana squash); zomorrod chalow (lamb stew); beef shish kebab.

Other recommendations: Chicken tandoori; aush (vegetable noodle soup); tabbouleh; borta (garlic-baked eggplant); mantu (pasta filled with ground beef).

Summary & comments: Though the menu is full of riches and surprises, you need to be careful about ordering lest you end up with five items but only two tastes. Appetizers are especially wonderful, particularly the sambosas, meat dumplings, and almost anything with eggplant. Stews dominate the entrees, and dishes with lamb hold up best. Because so much is long and slowly cooked, it almost doesn't make a difference that many of the vegetables start out canned or frozen.

Kung Food
Vegetarian Restaurant

Zone 6   Downtown/Uptown/Central
2949 Fifth Avenue
298-7302

International/Vegetarian
★★
Inexpensive

Quality 72   Value B

Reservations:	Accepted only during peak hours
When to go:	Lunch
Entree range:	$6–10
Payment:	VISA, MC, D
Service rating:	★★
Friendliness rating:	★
Parking:	Free lot
Bar:	None
Wine selection:	House
Dress:	Informal
Disabled access:	Yes
Customers:	Locals, businesspeople, visitors/tourists
Brunch:	Saturday and Sunday, 8:30 A.M.–1 P.M.
Lunch:	Every day, 11:30 A.M.–5 P.M.
Dinner:	Sunday–Thursday, 5–9 P.M.; Saturday and Sunday, 5–10 P.M.

Atmosphere/setting: Pretty much bare bones and diner looking, with plastic booths, formica table tops, and travel posters on the wall. An outside dining area is almost always available, although there's an industrial aura about it.

House specialties: Greek spinach pie; spaghetti with mock sausage; lentil-walnut loaf; curried vegetables; mushroom-basil stroganoff; mock chicken-salad sandwich.

Other recommendations: Garden burger; nachos supreme; stuffed grape leaves; layered tofu supreme; steamed vegetables; Spanish omelet.

Summary & comments: Kung Food probably qualifies as the grand lima bean of vegetariana in San Diego. It attracts vegans, dieters, the curious, and the politically correct. The menu is mostly devoted to Old Wave vegetarian dishes—salads, sprouts, shepherd's pie—but ingredients is always fresh and the range of grains, tofu, rice milks, and vegetable juices is very broad. There's an earnestness about the place that's so pervasive it seems to cause diners to speak only in quiet tones about weighty topics.

Honors & awards: Best Vegetarian Restaurant, *San Diego Magazine;* One of Our Favorite Breakfasts in San Diego, *Union Tribune.*

LA COSTA

Zone 8	Coronado /
	South Bay / Tijuana
Calle 7 No. 1831,	
Tijuana (7th Street, between	
Revolución and Constitución,	
downtown)	
011-52-66-85-8494	

<table>
<tr><td>Mexican / Seafood</td></tr>
<tr><td>★ ★ ★</td></tr>
<tr><td>Moderate</td></tr>
<tr><td>Quality 87   Value B</td></tr>
</table>

Reservations:	Accepted
When to go:	Lunch or dinner
Entree range:	$9–16
Payment:	VISA, MC
Service rating:	★ ★
Friendliness rating:	★ ★ ★
Parking:	Street
Bar:	Full service
Wine selection:	Limited
Dress:	Dressy casual
Disabled access:	Yes
Customers:	Locals, businesspeople, visitors / tourists
Open:	Every day, 10 A.M.–midnight

Atmosphere / setting: La Costa is very familiar terrain and that makes it immediately comfortable. There's a smoking and a nonsmoking side in this large restaurant, and both areas are trimmed with oak and have fairly low ceilings. There are a few booths, but mostly the rooms are filled with solid and functional wood tables and chairs.

House specialties: Shrimp, available in 17 different preparations; squid, in 7 preparations; oysters in 8. Whole baked fish; shrimp soup.

Other recommendations: Squid with garlic and oil; ceviche; grilled sea bass; seafood brochette; grilled shrimp.

Summary & comments: In addition to the standard preparation of fish and seafood which La Costa expects to have available daily, there's a "fresh fish" category of the menu which depends entirely on the catch of the day. Whatever the fish happens to be (sea bass and red snapper are common), it's available in several different preparations. Virtually all entrees are served as complete and very filling meals that begin with an appetizer—usually small pieces of fried fresh fish—followed by a seafood soup, entree, and dessert. Dessert is an incredibly caloric (and wonderful) concoction of melted vanilla ice cream whipped with Kahlúa and crème de cocoa. From the border, La Costa is no more than a 5-minute drive or a 20-minute walk. It's in the center of the central tourist area.

La Strada

Zone 6 Downtown/Uptown/Central	Italian
702 Fifth Avenue	★★★
239-3400	Moderate
	Quality 88 Value C

Reservations:	Recommended
When to go:	Any time
Entree range:	$10–19
Payment:	VISA, MC, AMEX, DC, D
Service rating:	★★★
Friendliness rating:	★★
Parking:	Street, valet in the evenings
Bar:	Full service
Wine selection:	Good
Dress:	Dressy casual
Disabled access:	Yes
Customers:	Locals, businesspeople, visitors/tourists
Lunch:	Every day, 11:30 A.M.–4 P.M.
Dinner:	Sunday–Thursday, 4–11:30 P.M.;
	Friday and Saturday, 4 P.M.–1 A.M.

Atmosphere/setting: Very stylish ristorante: a large room filled with tables covered with white cloths and an open kitchen along the back wall. Wraparound glass windows look out onto the street. Small outdoor dining area.

House specialties: The best of the pasta is the homemade wide noodles with a ragout; vegetable pizza is an interesting concoction, almost like a pizza crudité; tiramisu is the second-best in town. (See Salvatore's for the very best.)

Other recommendations: String pasta with smoked salmon; penne with clams and shrimp; lamb chop with fresh herbs; chicken breast with artichoke hearts.

Summary & comments: Despite its sleek looks, the trendiest thing about La Strada are the moody waiters with shellacked-back hair. It's a place that hybridizes what's in style and what's not, and both food and service is multo matter-of-fact. What you order is what you get, without frills, nasturtiums, or baby vegetables. The abundance of windows adds to the smartness of the look and provides a wonderful opportunity for viewing the extraordinary parade passing along Fifth Avenue.

LAUREL

American/Continental

★★★★

Moderate

Quality 93   Value B

Zone 6   Downtown/Uptown/Central
505 Laurel Street
239-2222

Reservations:	Recommended
When to go:	Any time
Entree range:	Lunch, $9–13; dinner, $10–20
Payment:	VISA, MC, AMEX, DC, D
Service rating:	★★
Friendliness rating:	★★★
Parking:	Street, valet
Bar:	Full service
Wine selection:	Extensive
Dress:	Dressy casual
Disabled access:	No
Customers:	Locals, businesspeople
Lunch:	Monday–Friday, 11:30 A.M.–2:30 P.M.; Satruday and Sunday, closed.
Dinner:	Monday–Thursday, 5:30–10 P.M.; Friday–Sunday, 5–10 P.M.

Atmosphere/setting: A large open room with creamy walls and fixtures, a high ceiling, and a very urbane sensibility. A kinder and gentler vision of Manhattan.

House specialties: The menu changes often, but the tuna carpaccio or ahi tartare make frequent appearances on the appetizer list. Roasted wild boar; red pepper shellfish soup; salmon; pork loin.

Other recommendations: Provençal chicken in a clay pot; Moroccan lamb loin with couscous; braised veal shank; lightly smoked trout; pan-roasted sea bass.

Summary & comments: Simplicity, simplicity, simplicity seems to be the mantra here, but don't believe it for a moment. This is a simplicity based on complex intelligence, not naiveté. While many of the foods appear familiar and presentations are often modest and bistro-like, there is considerable creativity behind virtually every dish served. Laurel is one of those restaurants whose very look raises expectations about its food. Most of the time it delivers unflinchingly. Waiters wear khakis and striped shirts which take the edge off what's otherwise a formal and formidable-looking restaurant. The force behind the food is Chef Doug Organ who, though continuing to look like a Yale freshman, has developed an impressive reputation. A bar menu composed mostly of appetizers is available every evening for as late as anyone hangs out at the bar. Another restaurant Organ and a partner operate in Sorrento Mesa, the WineSellar and Brasserie, serves excellent food, but in no way compares to the uptown experience of Laurel.

Le Fontainebleau Room

	Continental
Zone 6 Downtown/Uptown/Central	★★★
Westgate Hotel, 1055 Second Avenue	Expensive
238-1818	Quality 88 Value C

Reservations:	Recommended
When to go:	Dinner
Entree range:	$19–26
Payment:	VISA, MC, AMEX, DC, D
Service rating:	★★★★
Friendliness rating:	★★
Parking:	Valet, validated parking
Bar:	Full service
Wine selection:	Extensive
Dress:	Dressy, business attire
Disabled access:	Yes
Customers:	Locals, businesspeople, visitors/tourists
Brunch:	Sunday, 10 A.M.–2 P.M.
Lunch:	Monday–Friday, 11:45 A.M.–2 P.M.; Saturday, closed.
Dinner:	Every day, 6–10 P.M.

Atmosphere/setting: Posh, elegant, French empire–style dining, with rich upholstery and ornate flourishes every place you look.

House specialties: Lobster bisque with scallops; escargot with burgundy butter; osso buco; rack lamb chops; monkfish Provençal; lobster and shrimp ravioli.

Other recommendations: Grilled veal chop with truffles; sautéed Dover sole; vegetable platter with risotto.

Summary & comments: A place where businesspeople and traditionalists flock, the Fontainebleau Room is located upstairs in what was originally designed as the most formal hotel in town. Because the restaurant is so wonderfully quiet, it's an ideal setting for business deals or quiet conversation among couples. The room is rarely crowded, small private dining areas are available, and though chefs change, a common denominator is the ability to handle meat especially well.

LE PEEP

Zone 1   North County Inland
13385 Poway Road, Poway
679-2006

Zone 2   North County Coastal
3545 Del Mar Heights Road
755-8008

Reservations:	Accepted
When to go:	Any time
Entree range:	$4–7
Payment:	VISA, MC, AMEX
Service rating:	★★★
Friendliness rating:	★★★
Parking:	Free lot
Bar:	None
Wine selection:	None
Dress:	Informal
Disabled access:	Yes
Customers:	Locals
Breakfast/Lunch:	Every day, 7:30 A.M.–2:30 P.M.

Atmosphere/setting: While the restaurant is large and set within a busy suburban shopping center, it's well divided into smaller eating areas and seems very much like a big and fussy mom-and-pop coffee shop with lattice decor and maple furnishings.

House specialties: Hobo Banquet (potatoes, onions, cheese, and eggs); Zapata frittata; banana-pecan pancakes; tuna steak sandwich; southwestern crêpes; pita stuffed with turkey, bacon, and Muenster cheese.

Other recommendations: BLT; barbecued chicken; Belgian waffles; garden omelet.

Summary & comments: Though there are dozens of Le Peeps across the country, there are only three in California. At this one near Del Mar, crowds are typically so thick you're sure they're giving food away. Since portions are large, seasonings are mild, and there's rarely any surprise, Le Peep is especially popular with families, teens, and seniors. The noise level is fairly high but few seem to mind because there's so much good humor about the place.

Little Tokyo

	Japanese
	★★
Zone 1 North County Inland	Inexpensive
11640 Carmel Mountain Road, Suite 122	
675-1468	Quality 76 Value B
Zone 6 Uptown/Downtown/Central	

501 University Avenue OB   *Now "Wami"*
291-8518

Reservations:	Not accepted
When to go:	Any time
Entree range:	$6–13
Payment:	VISA, MC
Service rating:	★★
Friendliness rating:	★★
Parking:	Free lot
Bar:	Limited
Wine selection:	House
Dress:	Informal
Disabled access:	Yes
Customers:	Locals
Open:	Monday–Saturday, 11 A.M.–10 P.M.;
	Sunday, 11 A.M.–9 P.M. (Carmel Mountain);
	Sunday–Thursday, 11 A.M.–10 P.M.;
	Friday and Saturday, 11 A.M.–11 P.M.
	(University)

Atmosphere / setting: It's a slightly upgraded fast-food environment with hard surfaces, bright lights, sprightly but spooky art, banquettes, and a few tables.

House specialties: Chicken bowl; beef bowl; udon; teriyaki chicken with tempura and salad; assorted tempura and sashimi.

Other recommendations: Vegetarian yaki udon; sushi bento (assorted sushi with teriyaki chicken and fruit); fried seafood mix; rice bowl with curried beef.

Summary & comments: Little Tokyo provides reliable and serviceable Japanese food in large portions at reasonable prices. Sushi is available, but it's not one of the best sellers in the house. Most people come for the combination plates, especially those featuring the teriyaki chicken or beef.

Los Arcos

	Mexican/Seafood
	★★★★
Zone 8 Coronado / South Bay / Tijuana	Inexpensive
Boulevard Salinas 1000, Tijuana	
011-52-66-86-3171 or 4757	Quality 90 Value A

Reservations:	Accepted but rarely necessary
When to go:	Any time
Entree range:	$5–8
Payment:	VISA, MC
Service rating:	★★
Friendliness rating:	★★
Parking:	Free lot, street
Bar:	Full service
Wine selection:	Limited
Dress:	Informal
Disabled access:	Yes
Customers:	Locals
Open:	Monday–Wednesday, 8 A.M.–10 P.M.; Thursday–Saturday, 8 A.M.–midnight; Sunday, closed.

Atmosphere / setting: Los Arcos has two very large rooms, with the one on the left just a bit bigger, sunnier, and more vibrant than the one on the right—probably because the room on the left has lots of skylights. Both have fish nets hanging from the ceiling, brightly painted chairs, and colorful table cloths.

House specialties: Ceviche tostadas; smoked marlin tacos; grilled fish zarandeado.

Other recommendations: Rosario oysters; tuna fish stew; fresh octopus; shrimp cocktails.

Summary & comments: There's a large menu and everything, unfortunately, is not uniformly delicious. But if you stick with the house specialties you'll swear it's the best seafood you've ever eaten. The ceviche tostadas and smoked marlin tacos are appetizers, so order at least one per person. The zarandeado is a whole fish, usually red snapper, that has the main bones removed; then it's opened, grilled with a few seasonings, and served on enormous platters. It's priced by the kilo, so you order for the number of people who'll be eating it, i.e., two, three, five, ten. Because the portions are large, you might consider ordering only three-quarters the number of people who'll actually be eating. It's extraordinarily delicious. To get there, take Agua Caliente four blocks past the bull ring, turn left, then left again on the one-way Boulevard Salinas. It's on the corner on the right. Or just take a taxi from the border.

Machupicchu

	Peruvian
	★★★
Zone 5 Mission Bay and the Beaches	Inexpensive
4755 Voltaire Street	
222-2656	Quality 80 Value B

Reservations:	Accepted
When to go:	Dinner
Entree range:	$7–11
Payment:	VISA, MC
Service rating:	★★★
Friendliness rating:	★★★
Parking:	Street
Bar:	Limited
Wine selection:	House
Dress:	Informal
Disabled access:	Yes
Customers:	Locals, visitors / tourists, ethnic
Dinner:	Monday, Wednesday, and Thursday, 5:30–8:30 P.M.; Friday, 5:30–10 P.M.; Saturday, 3–10 P.M.; Sunday, 3–8:30 P.M.; Tuesday, closed.

Atmosphere / setting: From the outside, it's a cozy-looking neighborhood storefront; inside, you'll find a setting that's both eccentric and low key. There are a dozen tables covered in red cloths over which is laid lace-patterned plastic. Half the seating is folding chairs, including the "booths." Wall decor is mostly photos of Machupicchu and several ceremonial plates. The ceiling is low and there's a smell of age.

House specialties: Ceviche mixto; papa rellena (stuffed potato); antichucos (grilled beef heart); pasta with a spinach and nut sauce; sea bass in garlic sauce; lamb stew.

Other recommendations: Shredded chicken in a cheese and nut sauce; grilled steak with onions and garlic; shrimp soup; chicken breast with a cottage cheese sauce.

Summary & comments: Pop cooks and mom serves in this wonderfully idiosyncratic little restaurant. Be sure to try the small and tasty cubes of beef heart that are grilled on a skewer and served either plain or with a variety of sauces. The excellent stuffed potato is filled with a mix of ground beef, pork, lamb, and spices. The entire menu is fascinating, portions are large, and you can't help but come away with the sense that you've received great value and fascinating food for your dining dollar.

Manhattan

	Italian
	★★★
	Moderate/Expensive
	Quality 88 Value C

Zone 3   La Jolla
Empress Hotel, 7766 Fay Avenue
554-1444

Reservations:	Recommended
When to go:	Dinner
Entree range:	Lunch, $7–13; dinner, $11–24
Payment:	VISA, MC, AMEX, DC, D
Service rating:	★★★
Friendliness rating:	★★★
Parking:	Valet, street
Bar:	Full service
Wine selection:	Extensive
Dress:	Business attire, dressy casual
Disabled access:	Yes
Customers:	Locals, businesspeople, visitors/tourists
Lunch:	Monday–Friday, 11:30 A.M.–2 P.M.; Saturday and Sunday, closed.
Dinner:	Every day, 5–10:30 P.M.

Atmosphere/setting: With its leatherette booths, brick walls, and no-nonsense attitude about food, Manhattan is comfortable and slightly moody, quiet, adult, and urbane. Waiters are in tuxedos.

House specialties: Manhattan features food like fried calamari with marinara, chicken piccata in a thick lemon-butter sauce dotted with huge capers, and battered and sautéed sole.

Other recommendations: Rack of lamb; seafood stew; pasta; steak.

Summary & comments: Often considered the best place locally for New York–style Italian food, Manhattan is almost quaint in its serious regard for hearty East Coast eating. Lots of customers seem to be regulars, and none of them mistake Manhattan as a place for cucina moderna.

Marine Room Restaurant

Zone 3 La Jolla	French
La Jolla Beach and Tennis Club,	★★
2000 Spindrift Drive	Moderate/Expensive
459-7222	Quality 79 Value C

Reservations:	Recommended
When to go:	Especially at sunset for cocktails, or any time when there's a high tide
Entree range:	Lunch, $8–12; dinner, $16–31
Payment:	VISA, MC, AMEX, DC, D
Service rating:	★★
Friendliness rating:	★★
Parking:	Free lot, valet, street
Bar:	Full service
Wine selection:	Extensive
Dress:	Business attire, dressy casual
Disabled access:	Yes
Customers:	Locals, businesspeople, visitors/tourists
Brunch:	Sunday, 10 A.M.–2:30 P.M.
Lunch:	Monday–Saturday, 11:30 A.M.–2:30 P.M.
Dinner:	Every day, 6–10 P.M.

Atmosphere/setting: There's a dining room to your right and to your left, but you're going to be transfixed by the view—which is of the Pacific Ocean virtually lapping at the windows in front of you. Waiters are in tuxedos and the tables are formally dressed.

House specialties: Escargot and chanterelles en croûte; salmon carpaccio; mock turtle soup; bouillabaisse; charbroiled Hawaiian swordfish; braised John Dory; venison medallions; duck with porcini risotto.

Other recommendations: Fresh oysters; lobster bisque; baked sea bass; free-range chicken on a hazelnut crêpe; prime rib.

Entertainment & amenities: Dancing Tuesday through Saturday.

Summary & comments: The Marine Room has been around for 50 years and the food has had its highs and lows—but it's been slowly moving up for more than a year since a new chef was installed. There's an old-fashioned, courtly quality to both preparations and service. The dining room is also fixed in local mythology not only because of the view, but because of ferocious waves that lash at the windows during storms. Several times in the last few decades, storm waves broke through and flooded the restaurant. Don't worry, though; when there's a storm likely, reservations are impossible to get.

Honors & awards: Five Star Diamond, Best Dining with a View.

149

MARIUS

French Provençal	
★★★★★	
Expensive / Very Expensive	
Quality 99	Value B

Zone 8   Coronado /
             South Bay / Tijuana
Le Meridien Hotel,
   2000 Second Street, Coronado
435-3000

Reservations:	Essential
When to go:	Any time
Entree range:	$40–50 fixed-price menu
Payment:	VISA, MC, AMEX, DC, D
Service rating:	★★★★★
Friendliness rating:	★★★★
Parking:	Free lot, valet
Bar:	Full service
Wine selection:	Extensive
Dress:	Dressy, dressy casual
Disabled access:	Yes
Customers:	Locals, visitors / tourists
Dinner:	Tuesday–Saturday, 6–10 P.M.; Sunday and Monday, closed.

Atmosphere / setting: Small, understated, elegant, quiet, and the most sophisticated dining room in town. It's just off the main hotel lobby.

House specialties: Rockfish soup with rouille; sautéed foie gras with caramelized apples; mille-feuille of lobster and sautéed sea scallops with mushroom salpicon; roasted pheasant on a bed of cabbage; crêpes filled with fig marmalade and porto sauce with pistachio ice cream.

Other recommendations: Cannelloni of Dungeness crab and Swiss chard; warm lobster salad; sautéed Pacific shrimp in a nest of basmati risotto; sautéed lamb chops and eggplant timbale.

Summary & comments: There's been an in-house attempt to take Marius down a peg or two, to make the prices of this lovely French Provençal restaurant more populist in the hopes of making it less a special-occasion place. The effort has been successful: there are now multi-course, fixed-price meals starting at $39, the labor-intensive preparation time has been reduced, and any stiffness has vaporized. Still, even in its modified form the restaurant soars. The day it opened Marius claimed title to being the most graceful and service-oriented restaurant in the region. It still is. Food is meticulously crafted, sensitively seasoned, and exquisitely presented. Broths literally sparkle with clarity, vegetables are young and perfectly formed, and fish, shellfish, poultry, and meats are predictably treated in extraordinary ways with exquisite care. All in all, a lush and noble experience.

Mille Fleurs

Zone 2 North County Coastal	French
6009 Paseo Delicias, Rancho Santa Fe	★★★★★
756-3085	Expensive / Very Expensive
	Quality 98 Value C

Reservations:	Essential
When to go:	Dinner
Entree range:	Lunch, $11–19; dinner, $24–32
Payment:	VISA, MC, AMEX, DC
Service rating:	★★★
Friendliness rating:	★★★
Parking:	Street
Bar:	Full service
Wine selection:	Extensive
Dress:	Dressy, dressy casual
Disabled access:	No
Customers:	Locals, visitors / tourists
Lunch:	Monday–Friday, 11:30 A.M.–2:30 P.M.; Saturday and Sunday, closed.
Dinner:	Sunday–Friday, 6–10 P.M.; Saturday, 5:30–10 P.M.

Atmosphere / setting: A quiet, elegant series of interconnecting rooms, one of which has the fireplace; all the rooms portray a sense of being sequestered from the world. Furnishings are generally country French and more serviceable than elaborate.

House specialties: Changes nightly. Examples include zucchini soup with curry and frog legs; layers of salmon, halibut, cucumbers, and potatoes with caviar lemon dressing; crisply sautéed Lake Superior whitefish on mashed potatoes with capers; grilled New York steak with Gorgonzola and merlot sauce.

Other recommendations: Cauliflower and potato soup; coq au vin; poached shrimp quenelles on angelhair pasta; veal loin Wiener schnitzel; lamb tenderloin on couscous.

Entertainment & amenities: Pianist on Thursday, Friday, and Saturday nights.

Summary & comments: Tucked into a courtyard of one of the most prestigious communities in San Diego County, Mille Fleurs exudes the sense of having arrived. Though the menu changes nightly, Chef Martin Woesle is restlessly creative and manages to be dependably and stunningly original. Presentations are so painstakingly crafted, you'll hesitate eating for fear of destroying a fine work of art—but you'll discover the taste is worth it.

Honors & awards: Top 25 National Restaurants, *Food & Wine;* Best French Restaurant, *San Diego Magazine.*

MILTON'S

Zone 2   North County Coastal
Flower Hill Mall,
   2660 Via de la Valle, Del Mar
792-2225

Deli
★★★
Inexpensive
Quality 80   Value B

Reservations:	Parties of 8 or more
When to go:	Any time
Entree range:	$7–13
Payment:	VISA, MC, AMEX
Service rating:	★★★
Friendliness rating:	★★★
Parking:	Free lot
Bar:	Limited
Wine selection:	House
Dress:	Informal
Disabled access:	No
Customers:	Locals, businesspeople
Open:	Sunday–Thursday, 7:30 A.M.–9 P.M.;
	Friday and Saturday, 7:30 A.M.–10:30 P.M.

Atmosphere / setting: Located in the Flower Hill Mall, this is a large restaurant with very high ceilings and, for a deli, very modern and sophisticated decor. It owes more to Beverly Hills than the Lower East Side, but that's only testimony to how far corned beef on rye has come. The booths are cushy and all the tables are covered with green cloths with butcher paper on top. Old-fashioned phones sit next to most of the booths, but you can only make 800 or credit-card calls. If there's a choice, ask to be seated in the front room, which is more in the center of things.

House specialties: Mish mosh soup; corned beef on rye; Romanian skirt steak; baked salmon; triple-decker sandwiches; liver and onions.

Other recommendations: Grilled herb eggplant; baby-back ribs; Louisiana-style fried shrimp; tuna melt; bacon cheeseburger; pork chop sandwich.

Summary & comments: Recently-transplanted New Yorkers and Chicagoans are less than enthusiastic about local deli options, but long-time residents know an opportunity when they taste it—and in the North Coastal area there are no other choices for deli. Milton's has been open about two years and it's stirred up about as much controversy as a restaurant can (those who hate it because it's nontraditional and those who love it because it's there are squadrons of about the same size), but it's been crowded almost all day long since the beginning. In addition to the restaurant, there's a deli counter at the front where meats, fish, breads, and pastries are available for takeout.

Monsoon Bombay

		International / Vegetarian
Zone 6	Downtown / Uptown / Central	★★★
		Inexpensive
3975 Fifth Avenue		
298-3155		Quality 82 Value B

Reservations:	Not accepted
When to go:	Any time
Entree range:	$4–6
Payment:	VISA, MC
Service rating:	★★
Friendliness rating:	★★★
Parking:	Street, validated parking
Bar:	None
Wine selection:	None
Dress:	Informal
Disabled access:	Yes
Customers:	Locals, businesspeople
Open:	Every day, 10 A.M.–9 P.M.

Atmosphere / setting: Located on the front side of a new art house cinema complex, Monsoon is all clean lines and modern sensibilities, with black and steel furnishings and an indoor waterfall. There's an outdoor patio as well.

House specialties: Lentil soup; falafel pocket; veggie burger; tabbouleh; vegetable lasagna; tofu curry; black-eyed pea curry; zucchini and mushroom curry; spinach pie.

Other recommendations: Vegetable pie; Thai pasta salad; stir fry over rice.

Summary & comments: This is a family-run business where you order at the counter and they deliver food to your table. It's one of the more interesting local vegetarian restaurants because in addition to the set menu, there's a lot of fiddling going on with daily specials. Most foods come with a bit of heat, though the friendly (if somewhat easily distracted) staff knows the food well enough to reliably guide newcomers. The vegetarian burger is excellent, as is the spicy lentil soup. Samosas are unexceptional.

Montanas American Grill

Zone 6 Downtown/Uptown/Central	American
1421 University Avenue	★★★★
297-0722	Inexpensive/Moderate
	Quality 93 Value B

Reservations:	Recommended
When to go:	Any time
Entree range:	Lunch, $6–10; dinner, $6–16
Payment:	VISA, MC, AMEX, DC
Service rating:	★★
Friendliness rating:	★★★
Parking:	Street
Bar:	Full service
Wine selection:	Good
Dress:	Dressy casual
Disabled access:	Yes
Customers:	Locals, businesspeople
Lunch:	Monday–Friday, 11:30 A.M.–5 P.M.; Saturday and Sunday, closed.
Dinner:	Monday–Thursday, Sunday, 5–10 P.M.; Friday and Saturday, 5–11 P.M.

Atmosphere/setting: Woody, sleek, and stylish, like an Upper East Side restaurant for up-and-comers.

House specialties: Pork chops; rack of baby-back ribs; stuffed chiles with smoked tomato salsa; fettuccine with roasted garlic; grilled chicken breast sandwich with Montrachet; chocolate cake with caramel sauce.

Other recommendations: Pastas; chilis; sausage with wild rice.

Summary & comments: Functioning as the modern version of a chop house, Montanas serves lots of grilled meats and does it with a straightforward approach that sets the tone of this very American restaurant. Lots of marvels also come on the side as vegetables or potatoes or salsas, many of which emphasize smoky flavors. There's a large U-shaped bar near the front of the restaurant and two separate dining rooms, but neither one is significantly better than the other. It all gets noisy when crowded.

Mister A's

Zone 6 Downtown/Uptown/Central	Continental
2550 Fifth Avenue	★★★
239-1377	Moderate/Expensive
	Quality 80 Value C

Reservations:	Recommended
When to go:	Any time
Entree range:	Lunch, $9–13; dinner, $20–30
Payment:	VISA, MC, AMEX, DC
Service rating:	★★★
Friendliness rating:	★★
Parking:	Valet, street
Bar:	Full service
Wine selection:	Extensive
Dress:	Dressy, business attire
Disabled access:	Yes
Customers:	Locals, businesspeople, visitors/tourists
Lunch:	Monday–Friday, 11:30 A.M.–2:30 P.M.; Saturday and Sunday, closed.
Dinner:	Every day, 5:30–10:30 P.M.

Atmosphere/setting: On the top floor of a mid-rise building across from Balboa Park, Mister A's has the look of an old-fashioned "good restaurant": wood paneling, chandeliers, floral carpeting, napery, waiters in tuxedos, and soft lights.

House specialties: Rack of lamb; whole Dover sole; roast tenderloin of beef; veal chop; flaming sword of chicken; filet mignon; and lobster tail.

Other recommendations: Steak Armagnac; Long Island duckling; Château-briand; fillet of sturgeon casserole.

Summary & comments: More than a decade ago, Mister A's was considered the top dining experience in town. It's still ranked high among those whose preference runs to Beef Wellington and classic sauces. There's a nightly five-course dinner for $20. One of the best reasons for Mister A's longevity are the views, which offer a wonderful panorama of much of San Diego. It's especially fine of Balboa Park, where the canopy of trees is pierced by an illuminated California Tower. On the other side of the room, there's an intriguing sweep of downtown and the airport. The bar is a perfect place to be at sunset.

Honors & awards: Four Diamond Award, American Automobile Club; *Wine Spectator* Grand Award and Award of Excellence; Three Star Award, California Restaurant Writers.

Mr. Chow's

Zone 4   Mission Valley and the Mesas
4619 Convoy Street
268-9638

Chinese Noodle House	
★★	
Inexpensive	
Quality 72	Value B

Reservations: Not accepted
When to go: Lunch
Entree range: $4–6
Payment: Cash only
Service rating: ★★
Friendliness rating: ★
Parking: Free lot
Bar: None
Wine selection: None
Dress: Informal
Disabled access: Yes
Customers: Locals
Open: Tuesday–Sunday, 11 A.M.–8 P.M.; Monday, closed.

Atmosphere / setting: This is your basic, no-nonsense laborer's lunchroom, with vinyl tile on the floor, formica tables, and serviceable chairs. A few Chinese prints are on the wall and, like virtually everything in the room, they're fading.

House specialties: Pan-fried dumplings; boiled pork and chive dumplings; shredded pork noodle soup; shrimp noodle soup; pickled radish; shredded seaweed salad; stewed bean cake.

Other recommendations: Dahn-dahn noodles; deluxe noodle soup; Mandarin-style cold noodles.

Summary & comments: "Nothing fancy" may not be emphatic enough. Straightforward, utilitarian dining is the order of the day in this noodle house, where the most common request is for one of the big bowls of steaming soup that are served brimming with noodles, meat/poultry/seafood, and vegetables. Terrific potstickers are available either steamed or fried, and the odd assortment of appetizers—like slices of cold beef—make it clear that Mr. Chow's roots are with the workers of the world.

Niban Japanese Restaurant

Zone 4   Mission Valley and the Mesas
7081 Clairemont Mesa Boulevard
268-0465

Japanese
★★
Inexpensive

Quality 79   Value A

Reservations:	Not accepted
When to go:	Any time
Entree range:	$5–7
Payment:	Cash only
Service rating:	★★
Friendliness rating:	★★
Parking:	Free lot
Bar:	Limited
Wine selection:	Saké only
Dress:	Informal
Disabled access:	Yes
Customers:	Locals, businesspeople
Lunch:	Monday–Saturday, 11:15 A.M.–2:30 P.M.; Sunday, closed.
Dinner:	Every day, 5–9:30 P.M.

Atmosphere/setting: A pleasantly done fast-food setting, with a counter in front where you place your order, and small tables and narrow booths where your lunch or dinner is delivered.

House specialties: Vegetable sukiyaki; mixed sushi; pork teriyaki; Bento combinations; oyako-don (chicken) bowl.

Other recommendations: Ginger seafood; mixed sashimi; fried gyoza; fried salmon.

Summary & comments: A perfect place for those looking for a clean and tidy Japanese restaurant serving large portions of unusually good food that's inexpensively priced. Most of the dishes are rather basic, but there's an impressive number of combinations available. There are indoor and outdoor tables, but indoor is nicer since all there is to look at outside is a parking lot.

157

Old Town Mexican Cafe

	Mexican
	★ ★ ★
	Inexpensive
	Quality 84 Value B

Zone 6   Downtown/Uptown/Central
2489 San Diego Avenue
297-4330

Reservations:	Only for parties of 10 or more
When to go:	Any time, but especially dinner
Entree range:	$5–11
Payment:	VISA, MC, AMEX, D
Service rating:	★ ★
Friendliness rating:	★ ★ ★
Parking:	Free lot (but it's small), street
Bar:	Full service
Wine selection:	Good
Dress:	Informal
Disabled access:	Yes
Customers:	Locals, visitors/tourists
Open:	Every day, 7 A.M.–11 P.M.

Atmosphere/setting: A spacious restaurant with a few booths and mostly rough-carved tables and chairs. Everything you'd want in a bustling cantina is here, including an area up front where tortillas are made by hand.

House specialties: Carnitas; rotisserie chicken and ribs; handmade tortillas; margaritas.

Other recommendations: Chicken taco salad; carne asada taco; suprema tostadas; huevos rancheros; steak picado.

Summary & comments: It always feels like there's a party going on at Old Town Mexican Cafe, and that's not far from the truth: there are likely dozens happening simultaneously. The good cheer is contagious, though the noise level can make it difficult to hear the person across the table. The signature dish is carnitas—shredded pork served with salsa, cilantro, onions, peppers, and tortillas—and you roll your own. It's a terrific dish for a group, made perfect by a cold cerveza. There's almost always a crowd, so expect to wait for a table.

Honors & awards: Gold Medallion, San Diego Restaurant Association; *San Diego Magazine* Readers' Poll, Best Mexican.

Old Town Thai

<table>
<tr><td>Zone 6   Downtown/Uptown/Central
2540 Congress Street
291-6720</td><td>Thai
★★★
Inexpensive

Quality 80   Value B</td></tr>
</table>

Reservations:	Accepted
When to go:	Any time
Entree range:	$5–8
Payment:	VISA, MC
Service rating:	★★
Friendliness rating:	★★★★
Parking:	Street
Bar:	Limited
Wine selection:	House
Dress:	Informal
Disabled access:	Yes
Customers:	Locals, visitors/tourists
Lunch:	Tuesday–Sunday, 11 A.M.–4 P.M.; Monday, closed.
Dinner:	Tuesday–Sunday, 5–10 P.M.; Monday, closed.

Atmosphere/setting: It's a small wood-framed house that's clearly seen better days. Outside is a raised concrete patio set with a half-dozen tables, and inside is an L-shaped room, minimally decorated, with another half-dozen tables. There's a bathtub in the ladies room, but I think it's mostly for decoration.

House specialties: Hot and sour soup with lemongrass; garlic shrimp divine; Siamese shrimp; pad thai; chicken rice in earthen pot.

Other recommendations: Chicken salad; spicy barbecued beef salad; vegetarian curry; pan-fried noodles with beef; dry curry with ginger, garlic, and beef.

Summary & comments: Though your first thought might be that you haven't eaten in a place like this since your student days, persevere. Old Town Thai offers distinctive Thai cooking which might share the name of dishes served elsewhere, but will bear little relation. The pad thai and chicken hot pot are excellent, as is the cold beef salad. If you don't like spicy food, it's probably a good idea to tell the server to leave out all chiles. The kitchen doesn't seem to be able to tell the difference between mild and hot, so you're better off going for one extreme or the other.

Ole Madrid

Spanish / Mediterranean
★★
Moderate

Quality 75   Value D

Zone 6   Downtown / Uptown / Central
755 Fifth Avenue
557-0146

Reservations:	Recommended
When to go:	Happy hour and weekend evenings
Entree range:	$5–30
Payment:	VISA, MC, AMEX, DC, D
Service rating:	★★
Friendliness rating:	★★
Parking:	Fee lot, valet, street
Bar:	Full service
Wine selection:	Good
Dress:	Dressy casual, informal
Disabled access:	Yes
Customers:	Locals, visitors / tourists
Lunch:	Every day, 11:30 A.M.–4 P.M.
Dinner:	Every day, 4 P.M.–midnight

Atmosphere / setting: Three distinct seating areas occupy three levels in a wonderfully theatrical interpretation of an ancient eating house in Spain. The rooms are narrow but the ceiling arches 20 feet over you; wine-red velvet drapes separate rooms; curving staircases head off in different directions, though one of them leads to the stage where the flamenco is performed. The walls are brightly painted in dusty colors, wood planks cover the floor, and the larger tables—though not the action—is in the room with Picasso's Guernica on the wall.

House specialties: Roasted garlic consommé; tortilla Española; shrimp, octopus, and mussels with sweet peppers; trout with olive oil; chicken in roasted garlic sauce; tiger shrimp stuffed with peppers; paella (vegetarian and seafood); rabbit loin stuffed with mushrooms; tuna in a tomato sauce.

Other recommendations: Filet with Roquefort cream; roast chicken with sweet peppers and ham; salmon with fruit salsa; shellfish in a tomato almond sauce.

Entertainment & amenities: Flamenco dance performance on Thursday, Friday, and Saturday nights. Also reggae and jazz bands on weekends.

Summary & comments: Though virtually empty at lunchtime, Ole Madrid fills up most evenings and swells on the weekends with wall-to-wall bodies. Tapas are good, but tend to be overpriced; dinnertime entrees are a better value. Best of all, go at happy hour when all the tapas are half price.

150 Grand Café

Zone 1   North County Inland
150 West Grand Avenue, Escondido
738-6868

Reservations:	Recommended
When to go:	Lunch or dinner
Entree range:	$10–18
Payment:	VISA, MC, AMEX, DC
Service rating:	★★
Friendliness rating:	★★
Parking:	Free lot, street
Bar:	Full service
Wine selection:	Extensive
Dress:	Dressy casual, informal
Disabled access:	Yes
Customers:	Locals, businesspeople
Lunch:	Monday–Saturday, 11:30 A.M.–4:30 P.M.; Sunday, closed.
Dinner:	Every day, 4:30–9 P.M.

Atmosphere / setting: Set on the main street in central Escondido, 150 Grand has a panel of windows in front that lets passersby look in on diners. Of the two rooms in the restaurant, the smaller one on the left holds the bar and a number of tables, but it's more informal and feels like lunch; on the right, the room with the fireplace, library shelves, and very comfortable booths feels much more like dinnertime.

House specialties: Daily lunch and dinner specials; hamburgers with smoked Gouda and bacon; linguine with Dijon cream sauce sprinkled with salmon, dill, and tomato; littleneck clams with pesto and sundried tomatoes; flash-grilled tuna salad.

Other recommendations: Grilled poblano chile; polenta with shiitake mushrooms and pesto vinaigrette; grilled pork chops; duck in a dried cherry glaze; rock shrimp pasta.

Summary & comments: A lively cosmopolitan restaurant in the heart of downtown Escondido is unexpected, but that's where you'll find 150 Grand. It's small, bright, and cheery, with a limited but ambitious menu. Seasonings tend to the timid, but there's invariably a side sauce, relish, or flavored butter to perk things up. When the menu lists a sauce that's optional with a dish, always order it.

Honors & awards: *San Diego Home / Garden Magazine,* Silver Fork Award; *Entertainer Magazine,* Best Continental, Best Wine List, Best New North County Inland 1994.

Oscar's

Zone 1   North County Inland
12045 Carmel Mountain Road
592-0222

Zone 2   North County Coastal
1505 Encinitas Boulevard, Encinitas
632-0222

Zone 4   Mission Valley and the Mesas
3590 Rio San Diego Drive
295-6200

Reservations:	Not accepted
When to go:	Any time
Entree range:	$4–10
Payment:	VISA, MC, AMEX
Service rating:	★★
Friendliness rating:	★★
Parking:	Free lot
Bar:	None
Wine selection:	None
Dress:	Informal
Disabled access:	Yes
Customers:	Locals
Open:	Sunday–Thursday, 10:30 A.M.–9 P.M.;
	Friday and Saturday, 10:30 A.M.–10 P.M.

Atmosphere / setting: Large but modest setting; it's bright, clean, tidy, and rather garishly decorated in yellow and black.

House specialties: Greek salads; grilled chicken; barbecued ribs; pizza.

Summary & comments: Informal, unpretentious, and fast-foodish, Oscar's first brings people in with its fat, hot, garlicky, soft breadsticks. They're a bit greasy, but awfully good. Then they hang around for the Greek salads (served in yellow plastic bowls), barbecued or lemon chicken, baby-back ribs, or a half-dozen unusual pizzas. The Greek salads and the chicken are the biggest hits of all (next to the bread sticks), and the informality is so replete that a tantrum-throwing two-year-old probably wouldn't be noticed.

PACIFICA DEL MAR

Zone 2   North County Coastal
Del Mar Plaza,
   1555 Camino Del Mar, Del Mar
792-0476

Seafood/Fusion	
★★★★	
Moderate	
Quality 94	Value C

Reservations:	Recommended
When to go:	Any time
Entree range:	Lunch, $6–10; dinner, $9–19
Payment:	VISA, MC, AMEX, DC, D
Service rating:	★★★
Friendliness rating:	★★★
Parking:	Fee lot but validated, street, valet
Bar:	Full service
Wine selection:	Extensive
Dress:	Dressy casual, informal
Disabled access:	Yes
Customers:	Locals, visitors/tourists
Brunch:	Sunday, 10 A.M.–4 P.M.
Lunch:	Every day, 11 A.M.–4 P.M.
Dinner:	Every day, 4–10:30 P.M.

Atmosphere/setting: Pacifica Del Mar is large and modern, warm and smart, and most of all, urbane. There's a large bar as you enter and three separate dining areas. The patio is typically the preferred location, but no matter where you sit, it's all as cheery and chatty as a TV commercial full of people loving life.

House specialties: Shrimp and shiitake pot stickers with citrus glaze; warm goat cheese salad with cornmeal-crusted tomatoes; sea bass with ginger vinaigrette and tomato risotto; mustard chicken with mashed potatoes; wok-charred catfish; grilled, sugar-spiced, barbecued king salmon.

Other recommendations: Broiled pork chop with tomatillo cream sauce; blackened shrimp salad; cornmeal-fried calamari with chipotle aïoli.

Summary & comments: There's a happy hour food and bar menu with reduced prices 4–7 P.M. daily and reduced priced dinners every Monday 4–6:30 P.M. This place is very hip (but in a nonthreatening adult way) and always hopping. Chef Jackie Sloan-Donaldson is a creative force and passionate source of inventive and savory dining. She has a way with desserts so seductive you're willing to tempt fate and devour the entire sampler plate all by yourself. Sitting out on the patio on a soft summer evening, you can almost feel the membrane of the pleasure dome.

Honors & awards: Silver Fork Award, *San Diego Home/Garden Magazine;* Gold Medallion for Seafood, Southern California Restaurant Writers Association.

PALENQUE

Zone 5 Mission Bay and Beaches	Mexican
1653 Garnet Avenue	★★★
272-7816	Inexpensive / Moderate
	Quality 80 Value B

Reservations:	Only accepted on weekends or for parties of 4 or more
When to go:	Evenings
Entree range:	$8–15
Payment:	VISA, MC, AMEX, DC, D
Service rating:	★★
Friendliness rating:	★★★
Parking:	Free lot, street
Bar:	Limited
Wine selection:	House
Dress:	Dressy casual
Disabled access:	Yes
Customers:	Locals, visitors / tourists
Lunch:	Tuesday–Saturday, 11:30 A.M.–2:30 P.M.; Sunday and Monday, closed.
Dinner:	Sunday–Thursday, 5–9 P.M.; Friday and Saturday, 5–10 P.M.

Atmosphere / setting: Set mid-block in its Pacific Beach neighborhood, Palenque resembles a restaurant at a Mexican seaside resort in a slightly funky way. The decor is composed mostly of Mexican tiles, mirrors, plants, and even an old brick oven left over from the days when this was a chicken takeout shop.

House specialties: Tinga poblana (finely shredded pork with chiles, chorizo, tomatoes, and potatoes); nopalitos (cactus salad); chicken with annatto seed and orange juice; chiles en Nogada (poblanos stuffed with beef, nuts, and candied fruit).

Other recommendations: Chicken mole poblano; paella; machaca (shredded beef, eggs, and salsa); poblano stuffed with beef, potatoes, capers, and raisins; enchiladas Morelia style; sincronizada (tortillas filled with grilled ham and cheese).

Summary & comments: Owner / chef Marialuisa Vilchis, trained as an architect, has been providing San Diego with unusual dishes from southern and central Mexico for eight years. Few menu items are found elsewhere in town, and she pushes possibilities even further on weekends when she makes special dishes. When the movie *Like Water for Chocolate* arrived, Palenque duplicated foods from the film and held *Chocolate* dinners. They're still available with an advance request. Be advised that service is slow and food can be spicy.

Panda Inn

Zone 6   Downtown/Uptown/Central
506 Horton Plaza
233-7800

Chinese
★★★
Inexpensive/Moderate
Quality 80   Value C

Reservations:	Recommended
When to go:	Any time
Entree range:	Lunch, $7–10; dinner, $8–20
Payment:	VISA, MC, AMEX, DC, D
Service rating:	★★★
Friendliness rating:	★
Parking:	Fee lot, but restaurant validates
Bar:	Full service
Wine selection:	House
Dress:	Dressy casual, informal
Disabled access:	Yes
Customers:	Locals, visitors/tourists
Open:	Sunday–Thursday, 11 A.M.–10 P.M.;
	Friday and Saturday, 11 A.M.–10:30 P.M.

Atmosphere/setting: Located in the restaurant area at the top of Horton Plaza shopping center, the Panda is upscale and modern, with clean lines and long sight distances. There's a bar and waiting area to the right as you walk in; straight ahead are alcoves fitted with booths. What you can't see is the large greenhouse-like room in the back which is filled with many tables and chairs and virtually doubles the size of the restaurant.

House specialties: Braised beef with tangerine peel; minced chicken on lettuce leaves; Panda shrimp; lemon scallops; sizzling seafood; aromatic chicken with eggplant; spicy beef.

Other recommendations: Honey-walnut shrimp; barbecued pork and pan-fried noodles; shrimp in lobster sauce; shredded beef with green pepper; braised whole sole; crisp duckling.

Summary & comments: Restaurants come and go at an alarming rate in downtown's justifiably celebrated Horton Plaza shopping center, but the Panda has been there since the beginning (that's more than a decade now) and it still reverberates with success. The reason seems to be its ability to move surefootedly along the narrow line between authenticity and showbiz: it satisfies Chinese food traditionalists as well as visitors in leisure suits. At the end of every meal you're served the best fortune cookie in town, which gets that way by being dipped in white chocolate.

Panevino

Zone 6 Downtown/Uptown/Central	Italian
722 Fifth Avenue	★★★★
595-7959	Moderate
	Quality 93 Value D

Reservations:	Recommended
When to go:	Any time
Entree range:	$10–19
Payment:	VISA, MC, AMEX, DC
Service rating:	★
Friendliness rating:	★★
Parking:	Street, valet in the evening
Bar:	Limited
Wine selection:	Good
Dress:	Dressy casual
Disabled access:	Yes
Customers:	Locals, visitors/tourists
Lunch:	Monday–Friday, 11:30 A.M.–2:30 P.M.;
	Saturday and Sunday, closed.
Dinner:	Monday–Friday, 5–10 P.M.;
	Saturday and Sunday, 5 P.M.–midnight

Atmosphere/setting: It's small and noisy and brightly lit, there's no place to wait, and tables are so closely spaced that even skinny people can't pass between them. You're often closer to the person at the next table than the one at your own.

House specialties: Daily pasta specials; osso buco; swordfish with pine nuts; salmon ravioli; cannoli torte.

Other recommendations: Grilled chicken; linguine with crab; stuffed focaccia; calamari stuffed with crabmeat and sun-dried tomatoes; sautéed wild mushrooms.

Summary & comments: In a town inundated with Italian restaurants, Panevino is a delicious standout. What attracts a devoted following is the frenzy of the place (it feels like Rome or New York or any other place where a heavy urban pulse invades small restaurants) and the home-style Italian cooking. Food is served steaming and aromatic, nothing is too fancy, and everything is cared for. The most popular item in the house is undoubtedly the osso buco, a thick slice of veal shank slowly cooked until it's ready to fall off the bone. If it's not on the menu, ask for it. Fish is handled very well, too.

Pannikin's Brockton Villa

Zone 3 La Jolla	California
1235 Coast Boulevard	★★★
454-7393	Inexpensive / Moderate
	Quality 89 Value B

Reservations:	Accepted only for large parties 24 hours in advance
When to go:	Breakfast, brunch, lunch
Entree range:	$5–9 at lunch, $8–14 at dinner
Payment:	VISA, MC, AMEX, DC, D
Service rating:	★★
Friendliness rating:	★★★
Parking:	Street; fee lot validated at Ace Parking
Bar:	Limited
Wine selection:	House
Dress:	Informal
Disabled access:	No
Customers:	Locals, visitors / tourists
Breakfast:	Monday–Friday, 8 A.M.–noon
Brunch:	Saturday and Sunday, 8 A.M.–3 P.M.
Lunch:	Monday–Saturday, 11:30 A.M.–3 P.M.
Dinner:	Monday–Saturday, 5–8 P.M.; Sunday, 5–9 P.M.

Atmosphere / setting: Barely more than a weather-beaten cottage perched above La Jolla Cove, this cozy little bit of white clapboard offers spectacular ocean views. Though it's been restored a number of times, the fact that it was built in 1894 and used as a beach house most of the time since is evident in its worn, warm, and creaky character.

House specialties: Tower of bagels; French toast; turkey meat loaf sandwich; Reuben sandwich; grilled albacore with ginger cilantro butter; basil ravioli; grilled pork chops.

Other recommendations: Oatmeal; Greek steamers (eggs with feta); grilled shrimp and chicken salad; vegetable penne; chicken curry.

Summary & comments: It's as if the Brockton Villa was created first in memory, then realized in La Jolla. The setting recalls a place where the whole family stopped once on a long-ago vacation. Try the glorious orange-scented French toast or sandwiches of ahi or meat loaf with chutney. No matter how good any single element of Brockton Villa may be, it's the gestalt of the place that overtakes. It's all so unassuming, so funky and family and reasonably priced, it's as if all these perfect elements convened by accident. They didn't, of course, but it makes for a mirage that anyone can experience.

Pelly's

Zone 2   North County Coastal
Poinsettia Village Shopping Center,
    7110 Avenida Encinas, Suite 101,
    Carlsbad
431-8454

Seafood	
★★★	
Inexpensive	
Quality 80	Value B

Reservations:	Not accepted
When to go:	Any time
Entree range:	$5–8
Payment:	Cash or personal checks with ID
Service rating:	★★★
Friendliness rating:	★★★
Parking:	Free lot
Bar:	None
Wine selection:	None
Dress:	Informal
Disabled access:	Yes
Customers:	Locals
Open:	Every day, 10 A.M.–7 P.M.

Atmosphere/setting: It's hardly much of a setting since Pelly's is almost entirely a fish market, with a few tables squeezed inside the store and several more outside in the shopping center patio. Meals are served on paper plates.

House specialties: Char-grilled seafood plates: snapper, calamari, mahimahi, shark, halibut, sea bass, salmon.

Other recommendations: Shrimp, crab, ono seafood salads; clam chowder; grilled seafood sandwiches.

Summary & comments: While the setting is cordial and friendly, no one goes to Pelly's for atmosphere. Pelly's is all about fish, most of it locally caught and all of it sparklingly, glisteningly fresh. One or more of the owners is somewhere behind the counter all the time. Pick something from the menu or from the case at the front of the store, and they'll cook it to your direction—so long as grilling or sautéing is what you have in mind.

Peohe's

	Hawaiian-Style Seafood
Zone 8 Coronado / South Bay / Tijuana	★ ★ ★
	Moderate / Expensive
1201 First Street, Coronado	
437-4474	Quality 80 Value D

Reservations:	Recommended
When to go:	Any time
Entree range:	$18–28
Payment:	VISA, MC, AMEX, DC, D
Service rating:	★ ★ ★
Friendliness rating:	★ ★ ★
Parking:	Free lot
Bar:	Full service
Wine selection:	Extensive
Dress:	Dressy casual
Disabled access:	Yes
Customers:	Visitors / tourists
Brunch:	Sunday, 10:30 A.M.–2:30 P.M.
Lunch:	Monday–Saturday, 11:30 A.M.–2:30 P.M.
Dinner:	Sunday–Thursday, 5:30–9:30 P.M.; Friday, 5:30–10:30 P.M.; Saturday, 5–10:30 P.M.

Atmosphere / setting: The restaurant feels like it's floating on the water rather than merely abutting the Coronado waterfront, but that's part of its appeal. Peohe's (pronounced "Pee-oh-eeze") has extraordinary views to San Diego, as well as a bright and lively interior with ponds, bridges, and dining "pods."

House specialties: Coconut crunchy shrimp; coconut crunchy calamari; halibut mai'a (halibut sautéed with bananas and macadamia nuts); hot and spicy sea bass; prime rib; rack of lamb.

Other recommendations: Lobster bisque; lobster; barbecued shrimp; New York steak; pan-seared yellowfin tuna.

Entertainment & amenities: Piano on Friday and Saturday evenings.

Summary & comments: Though it feels distinctively touristy here, you can bet that a good number of the folks with pink umbrellas in their drinks are locals. The menu is predominantly fish, although it's been bolstered lately with meats and poultry. Peohe's liveliness (detractors call it hokiness) makes it especially popular for Sunday brunch and senior birthdays.

PHO PASTEUR

Zone 4   Mission Valley and the Mesas
7612 Linda Vista Road, #117
569-7515

Vietnamese	
★★★	
Inexpensive	
Quality 80	Value B

Reservations:	Accepted
When to go:	Any time
Entree range:	$4–13
Payment:	VISA, MC
Service rating:	★
Friendliness rating:	★
Parking:	Free lot
Bar:	Limited
Wine selection:	House
Dress:	Informal
Disabled access:	Yes
Customers:	Locals, ethnic
Open:	Sunday–Thursday, 9 A.M.–10 P.M.;
	Friday and Saturday, 9 A.M.–11 P.M.

Atmosphere / setting: Set in a neighborhood shopping center that has at least two other Vietnamese restaurants, Pho Pasteur's many tables are covered with pink cloths, and an ornate gilded arch separates two dining rooms. The room on the right is slightly nicer than the one on the left. A big-screen TV plays Vietnamese music videos loud enough to fill the entire restaurant and honey-colored faux-wood paneling is on most walls.

House specialties: Pho Pasteur, a beef-based soup with rice noodles. Plates of fresh vegetables along with meat, shellfish, or poultry are brought to the table and you add them to the soup.

Other recommendations: Satay ancient hot pot, a spicy broth to which you add bok choy, sliced beef, shrimp, and squid; onion steak; vegetable rice paper rolls with hot chile sauce; chicken in lemongrass; ground shrimp on sugar cane; sweet-and-sour vegetable soup with catfish.

Summary & comments: If you don't see the name Pho Pasteur at first, look for the sign that says Ánh Hồng Bo 7 Món. Inside you'll find yourself in a well-lit, frequently crowded restaurant patronized primarily by Vietnamese. The menu has 197 numbered items and the staff is only moderately useful in helping you understand how things work. When in doubt, put everything that interests you in the soup.

PIATTI

Zone 3 La Jolla	Italian
2182 Avenida de la Playa	★★★★
454-1589	Moderate
	Quality 92 Value C

Reservations:	Recommended
When to go:	Dinner, brunch
Entree range:	$7–16
Payment:	VISA, MC, AMEX
Service rating:	★★★
Friendliness rating:	★★★
Parking:	Street
Bar:	Full service
Wine selection:	Extensive
Dress:	Informal
Disabled access:	Yes
Customers:	Locals
Brunch:	Saturday and Sunday, 11 A.M.–5 P.M.
Lunch:	Every day, 11:30 A.M.–5 P.M.
Dinner:	Sunday–Thursday, 5–10 P.M.;
	Friday and Saturday, 5–11 P.M.

Atmosphere / setting: It's light, spacious, and pastel, customized to the casual and high-styled chic beloved by La Jollans. Piatti's has the rural look that only an urbanite could create.

House specialties: Chicken grilled under a hot brick; homemade sausage with polenta, spinach, and sautéed peppers and onions; white pizza with prosciutto, mushrooms, mozzarella, and roasted garlic; rolled pasta with wild mushrooms, spinach, and ricotta; cannelloni with roasted veal and beef.

Other recommendations: Sautéed calf's liver; grilled marinated steak; veal scaloppine with mushrooms; scrambled eggs with smoked salmon and mascarpone cheese; sautéed sweetbreads with mushrooms over scrambled eggs.

Summary & comments: Part of a very small California chain, this bistro-style Cal-Ital dining room is in an ever-so-slightly out of way place in La Jolla. At dinnertime, there's not much else going on along the street, but Piatti's is booming. Far more locals frequent the spot than anyone else, and sometimes there's so much table hopping it feels like a community wedding. Sunday breakfast / brunch is wildly popular and the homemade bread is excellent.

Pizza Nova

Italian / Pizza	
★★★	
Inexpensive	
Quality 80	Value C

Zone 4   Mission Valley and the Mesas
8650 Genesee #228
458-9525

Zone 5   Mission Bay and Beaches
5120 North Harbor Drive
226-0268

Zone 6   Downtown / Uptown / Central
3955 5th Avenue
296-6682

Reservations:	Recommended
When to go:	Any time
Entree range:	$6–10
Payment:	VISA, MC, AMEX, DC, D
Service rating:	★★★
Friendliness rating:	★★
Parking:	Free lot
Bar:	Limited
Wine selection:	Good
Dress:	Informal
Disabled access:	Yes
Customers:	Locals, businesspeople
Open:	Sunday–Saturday, 11 A.M.–closing time varies with each location and day of the week; call the particular restaurant for specific information.

Atmosphere / setting: The original Pizza Nova on Harbor Drive used to be a fish restaurant and still feels like one. It's an older building, multi-level, a little funky, with lots of bare wood and water views. The newer Novas are all different, but generally share a cool, spare, and modern sensibility.

House specialties: Chicken tequila fettuccine; Thai chicken pizza; chicken Caesar salad.

Other recommendations: Fettuccine with smoked salmon in a cream sauce; black bean chili; BLT pizza; prosciutto and goat cheese calzone.

Summary & comments: Pizza Nova is a local mini-chain of wood-fired designer pizza restaurants—though the designs are more akin to Bill Blass than Claude Montana, which is to say they are fairly classic and dependable, with very few on-the-edge combinations.

Honors & awards: *San Diego Magazine,* Best Pizza.

172

POINT LOMA SEAFOODS

		Seafood
Zone 5 Mission Bay and Beaches		★★
2805 Emerson Street		Inexpensive
223-1109		
		Quality 79 Value C

Reservations:	No
When to go:	Any time
Entree range:	$4–9
Payment:	Cash only
Service rating:	★★
Friendliness rating:	★★
Parking:	Free lot
Bar:	Limited
Wine selection:	Good
Dress:	Informal
Disabled access:	Yes
Customers:	Locals
Open:	Monday–Saturday, 9 A.M.–6 P.M.; Sunday, noon–6 P.M.

Atmosphere / setting: It's a fish market with a restaurant as a side business. Principal seating is outdoors.

House specialties: Fried shrimp, clams, fish, and calamari sandwiches; oysters; creamed herring; ceviche; smoked fish.

Other recommendations: Shrimp and crab Louis.

Summary & comments: Point Loma Seafoods has been around for more than 30 years, and there's a sense of barely controlled tumult about the place. You order at the counter, mill around the small market area with several dozen other patrons until your number is called, and then wedge your way to the counter to get your food. Meal in hand, you squeeze your way out to find a seat in the sun or at the adjacent covered patio. The restaurant/market is quite literally on the docks—where much of the fish comes from—and there's a smokehouse just behind the market where anyone can bring fresh fish and have it smoked. Loyal patrons swear Point Loma Seafoods has the freshest fish in town.

PREGO

Zone 4   Mission Valley and the Mesas
1370 Frazee Road
294-4700

Reservations:	Recommended
When to go:	Any time
Entree range:	$9–19
Payment:	VISA, MC, AMEX, DC
Service rating:	★★
Friendliness rating:	★★★
Parking:	Free lot, valet
Bar:	Full service
Wine selection:	Extensive
Dress:	Dressy casual
Disabled access:	Yes
Customers:	Locals
Brunch:	Sunday holidays (Mother's Day, Father's Day, Easter, etc.), 11:30 A.M.–3:30 P.M.
Lunch:	Monday–Friday, 11:30 A.M.–5 P.M.; Saturday and Sunday, closed.
Dinner:	Monday–Saturday, 5–11 P.M.; Sunday, closed.

Atmosphere / setting: A stylish Tuscan villa done with loads of Memphis decor, black marble tables, and fabulous light fixtures. Adult, sophisticated.

House specialties: Duck breast salad with mâche; smoked mozzarella and eggplant pizza; the simpler pastas, especially the peppered pasta with tomato, garlic, and basil; grilled pork chops. For light eating, try the antipasto misto.

Other recommendations: Marinated octopus; pizza with tomato, arugula, prosciutto, and garlic; flower-shaped pasta filled with spinach and ricotta, in a light tomato sauce; sliced steak with black olives and artichokes.

Summary & comments: One more link in a chain of stylish Italian restaurants, Prego is virtually the only place to eat if you want good, interesting food in Mission Valley. The young chef is full of passion and ideas, and her seasonal menus are captivating. Special wine dinners are done a few times a year, and that's when the kitchen soars. The rest of the time, it's just darn good. When crowded though, Prego tends to be noisy, and the only way to escape is if it's summertime and you're sitting on the outdoor patio.

Honors & awards: *Wine Spectator* Award of Excellence; *San Diego Home / Garden Magazine,* Silver Fork Award; *San Diego Union Tribune,* Creme de la Creme.

Prince of Wales Grill

	American
	★★★★
Zone 8 Coronado /	Expensive
South Bay / Tijuana	
Hotel del Coronado,	Quality 90 Value C
1500 Orange Avenue, Coronado	
522-8818	

Reservations:	Essential
When to go:	Any time
Entree range:	$18–30
Payment:	VISA, MC, AMEX, DC, D
Service rating:	★★★★
Friendliness rating:	★★
Parking:	Fee lot validated by restaurant
Bar:	Full service
Wine selection:	Extensive
Dress:	Dressy
Disabled access:	Yes
Customers:	Locals, visitors / tourists
Dinner:	Tuesday–Saturday, 6–10 P.M.; Sunday and Monday, closed.

Atmosphere / setting: Subject to extensive remodeling in 1995, the stodgy old Prince of Wales Grill has been reborn, and rather extraordinarily at that. What used to be red leather and dark wood is replaced by beige and gold upholstery and a sense of absolute opulence. It's theatrical—like *Dynasty* or some other extravagant soap—but utterly wonderful.

House specialties: Grilled Pacific prawns; lobster ravioli; broiled swordfish; mustard marmalade lamb chops; grilled prime New York steak; seared tarragon scallops.

Other recommendations: Broiled salmon; roasted pheasant breast; angelhair pasta with portobello mushrooms; oysters with Midori melon relish.

Summary & comments: Along with the room, the tired old menu has been thoroughly revamped, and the new focus is on very simple cooking and straightforward presentations—which is a surprise given the lavish quality of the room. Basically, you get a hunk of excellent quality fish, meat, or poultry that's been broiled or grilled. On the side is a relish, compote, or chutney to give the dish a present tense. Desserts tend toward the very down-home, like Tunnel o' Fudge Cake.

Rainwater's on Kettner

Zone 6   Downtown / Uptown / Central
1202 Kettner Boulevard
233-5757

Reservations:	Recommended
When to go:	Any time
Entree range:	Lunch, $10–15; dinner, $17–36
Payment:	VISA, MC, AMEX, DC
Service rating:	★★★★
Friendliness rating:	★★
Parking:	Free lot, valet, street
Bar:	Full service
Wine selection:	Excellent
Dress:	Business attire, dressy casual
Disabled access:	Yes
Customers:	Locals, businesspeople
Lunch:	Monday–Saturday, 11:30 A.M.–5 P.M.; Sunday, closed.
Dinner:	Every day, 5 P.M.–midnight

Atmosphere / setting: Woody, upper-end chop house on the second floor of an old warehouse and storage building. Nicely decorated, clubby environment.

House specialties: Prime beef; fresh seafood; live Maine lobster; prime T-bone; prime New York steak; prime rib; rack of lamb; veal chop; calves' liver.

Other recommendations: Three-cheese meat loaf; broiled swordfish; chicken Dijon; duck sausage fettuccine.

Summary & comments: For almost a decade, this was the only place for a good steak. Though steakhouses have proliferated over time, Rainwater's still ranks among the best. In pre-enlightenment days, Rainwater's would have been called A Man's Restaurant, and even now much of the clientele is still male; flowers and ferns are eschewed in favor of crisp linens and deep booths. At lunchtime particularly, Rainwater's gives all the evidence you'll ever need that it's one of the last gathering places of the power brokers. Martinis still get drunk regularly at lunch and dinner, and you can hear the sound of two hands shaking as deals get made. A private dining room / wine room is available for small dinner parties.

Honors & awards: *San Diego Magazine,* Best Steakhouse, since 1986; *Wine Spectator* Award of Excellence.

RANCHO VALENCIA RESTAURANT

Zone 2 North County Coastal	California French
Rancho Valencia Resort,	★★★★★
5921 Valencia Circle, Rancho Santa Fe	Expensive / Very Expensive
756-3645	Quality 95 Value B

Reservations:	Recommended
When to go:	Any time
Entree range:	Lunch, $9–14; dinner, $19–25
Payment:	VISA, MC, AMEX, DC
Service rating:	★★★★
Friendliness rating:	★★★★
Parking:	Free lot
Bar:	Full service
Wine selection:	Extensive
Dress:	Dressy, dressy casual
Disabled access:	Yes
Customers:	Locals, visitors / tourists
Breakfast:	Every day, 7–11:30 A.M.
Lunch:	Every day, 11:30 A.M.–6 P.M.
Dinner:	Every day, 6–9:30 P.M.

Atmosphere / setting: Just off the adobe tile courtyard that leads to the resort's reception area is this somewhat formal dining room with its whitewashed timber ceiling and an elegant country French charm. Fresh flowers are on the widely spaced tables, whitewashed wood chairs have deeply cushioned bottoms, and live plants fill the room. The beautifully landscaped grounds are visible from anywhere in the restaurant since much of the room is filled with doors made entirely of small-paned windows.

House specialties: Risotto of quail with crimini mushrooms; crab cake with artichoke petals; warm crispy sweetbreads with arugula and balsamic vinaigrette; seared ahi with sesame-seed crust; sautéed sea scallops with Japanese eggplant; grilled buffalo steak with green peppercorns; sautéed veal medallions.

Other recommendations: King crab and Mexican prawn cocktail; tri-color fettuccine with lobster; free-range chicken marinated in achiote; scaloppine of venison with celery root fritters; butternut squash ravioli.

Summary & comments: It's easy to fall in love here—but the object of your affection could just as easily be the setting and the food as your partner. That's because things seem to come together so nicely, so graciously. The environment is glorious—let's hope the Lord can afford similar groundskeepers and decorators— and the menu is filled with ingenious combinations that are beautifully executed. You'll appreciate the absence of pomp and arrogance among the staff.

Rhinoceros Cafe and Grill

	American
Zone 8 Coronado /	★★★
South Bay / Tijuana	Inexpensive / Moderate
1166 Orange Avenue, Coronado	
435-2121	Quality 85 Value B

Reservations:	Accepted
When to go:	Any time
Entree range:	$8–15
Payment:	VISA, MC, AMEX
Service rating:	★★
Friendliness rating:	★★
Parking:	Street
Bar:	Limited
Wine selection:	Good
Dress:	Dressy casual
Disabled access:	Yes
Customers:	Locals, visitors / tourists
Breakfast:	Tuesday–Sunday, 8–11 A.M.; Monday, closed.
Lunch:	Every day, 11 A.M.–3 P.M.
Dinner:	Every day, 4–9 P.M.

Atmosphere / setting: A large open room with high ceilings, black and white tiles on the floors, and a straightforward bistro look. A few original paintings hang on the walls. Tables are also set on the sidewalk for outdoor dining.

House specialties: Pasta primavera; New York steak; poached salmon penne with tomato and vodka; marinated chicken.

Other recommendations: Sandwiches are available only at lunch and include such combinations as meat loaf with jalapeños and salsa, and grilled fish.

Summary & comments: Orange Avenue is the main commercial street in Coronado. As you stroll along the street—a local pastime—Rhinoceros will invariably draw your attention by the boldness of its look. The restaurant has a cosmopolitan style that's reminiscent of San Francisco, and that's really what the food is all about. Service, however, is pretty much Southern Californian and may be too relaxed and/or uncertain.

Rubio's

Zone 1   North County Inland
763 Center Drive, San Marcos
745-2962

Zone 6   Downtown/Uptown/Central
901 Fourth Avenue
231-7731

Zone 7   San Diego East/East County
399 Magnolia Avenue, El Cajon
440-3325

Reservations:	Not accepted
When to go:	Any time
Entree range:	$2–5
Payment:	Cash only
Service rating:	★★
Friendliness rating:	★★★
Parking:	Free lot, street depending on location
Bar:	Limited
Wine selection:	House
Dress:	Informal
Disabled access:	Yes
Customers:	Locals
Open:	Hours vary by location. Generally six days a week, 11 A.M.–9 P.M. Call for details.

Atmosphere/setting: Most Rubio's are designed on the same stylish fast-food model—they're clean and brightly lit, green and white and oak will be found somewhere in the decor, and all the surfaces are hard (formica, tile) to allow for easy scrubbing. Seating is both in booths and at tables.

House specialties: Fish tacos; machaca (shredded beef and scrambled eggs); Pesky Combo (two fish tacos especial with beans and chips).

Other recommendations: Carnitas burrito; grilled-chicken Caesar salad; nachos grande; grilled mahi fish burrito.

Summary & comments: A local Cinderella story, Rubio's started as a single restaurant featuring fish tacos and met with so much success it developed into a chain of more than a dozen San Diego restaurants. Now they're opening units up the California coast. What started it all is the fish taco, a strip of fish fillet that is battered and fried, then served in a soft corn tortilla with salsa, white sauce, and cabbage. It's a local staple. There's also a newly introduced menu of low-fat Mexican food. Many locations; check the phone book for the location nearest you.

Ruth's Chris Steak House

	Steaks
Zone 6 Downtown/Uptown/Central	★★★★
1355 North Harbor Drive	Expensive/Very Expensive
233-1422	Quality 94 Value D

Reservations:	Recommended
When to go:	Any time
Entree range:	$17–39
Payment:	VISA, MC, AMEX, DC
Service rating:	★★★★
Friendliness rating:	★★★
Parking:	Valet, street
Bar:	Full service
Wine selection:	Extensive
Dress:	Dressy casual
Disabled access:	Yes
Customers:	Locals, businesspeople
Dinner:	Sunday–Thursday, 5–10 P.M.;
	Friday and Saturday, 5–10:30 P.M.

Atmosphere/setting: It's one large room on several levels, with closely spaced tables and a wall of windows looking out to San Diego Bay. Though the tableware and upholstery are meant to give the room a somewhat formal look, it doesn't quite come off. Instead, it feels like a really nice lunchroom.

House specialties: Beef steak: T-bone, porterhouse, New York, filet.

Other recommendations: Veal chops, lamb chops.

Summary & comments: There's so much activity and energy at Ruth's that it often seems like a victory rally for the high school football team. Though the size of any dish rarely relates to price (i.e., it's all expensive), the treatment of vegetables is chancy, and there's little or no accommodation to anyone interested in minimizing fat and cholesterol; all those concerns are beside the point. Ruth's is all about steak, and the steak at Ruth's is absolutely and unequivocally superb. It's the most delicious beef in San Diego. Meat's the thing here and nothing else matters—including service that's so rapid you can be in and out in an hour's time.

SAFFRON

Zone 6   Downtown/Uptown/Central
3731 India Street
574-0177

Thai/Chicken	
★★★	
Inexpensive	
Quality 86	Value A

Reservations: Not accepted
When to go: Any time
Entree range: $4–12
Payment: VISA, MC
Service rating: ★★★
Friendliness rating: ★★
Parking: Fee lot, street
Bar: Limited
Wine selection: None
Dress: Informal
Disabled access: Yes
Customers: Locals
Open: Monday–Friday, 10:30 A.M.–8:30 P.M.;
                        Saturday and Sunday, 11 A.M.–8 P.M.

Atmosphere/setting: Saffron is little more than a storefront with a counter and rotisserie of perpetually turning chickens. Tables and chairs are available next door, up a short flight of steps, for al fresco dining.

House specialties: Thai grilled chicken; noodle dishes; Thai salads; satay.

Summary & comments: A tiny, mostly carry-out restaurant, Saffron provides daily specials, annual specials, and one-time-only specials—and some of all of them are knockouts. Though it's easy to get diverted by the specials, people typically return to the traditional, mahogany-colored grilled chicken. With a tender, juicy, and dependably fine taste, it has a sweet-spicy aroma that calls like a siren. Besides, you'll love the pleasure of choosing among the five distinctive dipping sauces. Peanut is the local favorite. Any grilled chicken that isn't sold within an hour gets turned into Thai chicken salad (which is also wonderful). During the summer, Saffron makes up complete picnic baskets (food, utensils, plates); just call in advance to arrange a time for pick-up.

Honors & awards: Cancer Society, Best Chef; *San Diego Union Tribune,* Best Chicken; *San Diego Home/Garden Magazine,* Silver Fork.

Sally's

Zone 6   Downtown/Uptown/Central
Hyatt Regency Hotel, One Market Place
687-6080

Seafood/Mediterranean
★★★★
Moderate/Expensive

Quality 92   Value C

Reservations:	Recommended
When to go:	Lunch or dinner on a nice day when you can sit outside
Entree range:	Lunch, $7–13; dinner, $16–25
Payment:	VISA, MC, AMEX, DC, D
Service rating:	★★★
Friendliness rating:	★★
Parking:	Fee lot validated by restaurant; valet
Bar:	Full service
Wine selection:	Good
Dress:	Dressy casual
Disabled access:	Yes
Customers:	Locals, visitors/tourists
Lunch:	Every day, 11:30 A.M.–2:30 P.M.
Dinner:	Sunday–Thursday, 5:30–10 P.M.; Friday and Saturday, 5:30–11 P.M.

Atmosphere/setting: Sally's is a large and elegant glass and copper box set right on the waterfront. Interiors are very modern. Outside dining is available, and the choicest area is the narrow patio that looks out over the bay.

House specialties: Crab cakes; tuna loin salad; bouillabaisse; seared sea bass; halibut and napa cabbage; roasted rabbit; grilled sea scallops on corn pancakes (if available).

Other recommendations: Baked salmon; braised calamari; scallops and farfalle; rosemary chicken; potato gnocchi with shiitake and oyster mushrooms.

Entertainment & amenities: Jazz on Friday and Saturday evenings from 6 to 10 P.M. By advanced arrangement, a table for 12 can be set up in the kitchen with a specially prepared menu.

Summary & comments: Sally's looks like it might be the hangout of ambitious attorneys and folks with too much attitude, but its location between Seaport Village and the San Diego Convention Center actually means it serves a clientele that's just as often in T-shirts and shorts as Armani and Anne Klein II. The wonderfully creative young chef cooked for French President François Mitterand at the Elysée Palace. Here, he leans toward seafood and Spanish cuisine, but doesn't really limit the food to any single theme. If the day is sunny and bright, be sure to sit outside. Sally's most significant drawback is the interior noise level; on crowded nights, the sound level is too awesome for words.

Salvatore's

Zone 6   Downtown/Uptown/Central
750 Front Street
544-1865

Italian	
★★★	
Moderate	
Quality 81	Value C

Reservations:	Recommended
When to go:	Any time
Entree range:	Lunch, $8–12; dinner, $11–22
Payment:	VISA, MC, AMEX
Service rating:	★★★
Friendliness rating:	★★★★
Parking:	Validated parking underground
Bar:	Full service
Wine selection:	Extensive
Dress:	Dressy casual
Disabled access:	Yes
Customers:	Locals, visitors/tourists
Lunch:	Monday–Friday, 11 A.M.–2:30 P.M.;
	Saturday and Sunday, closed.
Dinner:	Every day, 5–10 P.M.

Atmosphere/setting: This is one of downtown's most undeniably beautiful restaurants. It is soft and restrained, done in pastels and white wood accents, and when the sunlight streams through the windows, the interior shimmers jewel-like. It's all very elegant.

House specialties: Eastern veal; fresh seafood; all pastas, breads, and pastries made on premises.

Other recommendations: Lasagna; angelhair pasta with fresh tomato and arugula; risotto with shrimp; grilled swordfish; grilled lamb chops; veal scaloppine.

Entertainment & amenities: Banquet facilities available.

Summary & comments: Food at Salvatore's is reliably good, but the menu holds few surprises. The truth is that even though the pastas are all homemade and some chicken dishes are excellent, none of it matches the loveliness of the setting. But in a town filled with tiramisu, the best is found here.

183

Sammy's California Woodfired Pizza

Zone 2   North County Coastal
12925 El Camino Road, Del Mar
259-6600

Zone 3   La Jolla
702 Pearl Street
456-5222

Zone 6   Downtown/Uptown/Central
770 4th Avenue
230-8888

Italian/Pizza
★★★★
Inexpensive/Moderate

Quality 90   Value B

Reservations:	Not accepted except for parties of 6 or more
When to go:	Any time
Entree range:	$8–10
Payment:	VISA, MC, AMEX, DC
Service rating:	★★★
Friendliness rating:	★★
Parking:	Free lot, street
Bar:	Limited
Wine selection:	House
Dress:	Informal
Disabled access:	Yes
Customers:	Locals, visitors/tourists
Open:	Every day, 11:30 A.M.–11 P.M.

Atmosphere/setting: All the Sammy's share a sense of informality and the handsome look of a modern pizza parlor created for the disposable income crowd: everything is neat and clean, with as much blond oak as can fit in.

House specialties: Caesar salad; barbecued chicken pizza; spicy chicken angelhair pasta; super messy sundae.

Other recommendations: Pizza: goat cheese, grilled zucchini eggplant, five cheese, spicy roasted peppers. Pasta: chicken sausage fettuccine, penne Gorgonzola.

Summary & comments: Somewhere between San Francisco and Los Angeles, in the carryings-on of Alice Waters and Wolfgang Puck, there came the culinary love child we know as designer pizzas. They have been propagated and popularized locally by Sammy's. Sammy's pizzas are chic and clever, but also down to earth and reasonable. The original Sammy's in La Jolla is a mob scene particularly on weekends, but the chumminess of the place makes it OK.

Honors & awards: *San Diego Magazine,* Best Pizza; *San Diego Home/Garden Magazine,* Best Salad; Gold Medallion, Best Casual Restaurant.

Sfuzzi

Zone 6   Downtown/Uptown/Central
340 Fifth Avenue
231-2323

Italian Bistro	
★★★	
Inexpensive/Moderate	
Quality 80 Value C	

Reservations:	Recommended
When to go:	Any time, though brunch and special wine dinners are especially good.
Entree range:	$7–11
Payment:	VISA, MC, AMEX, DC
Service rating:	★★
Friendliness rating:	★★
Parking:	Fee lot, street
Bar:	Full service
Wine selection:	Good
Dress:	Dressy casual
Disabled access:	Yes
Customers:	Locals, visitors/tourists
Brunch:	Saturday and Sunday, 11 A.M.–3 P.M.
Lunch:	Monday–Friday, 11 A.M.–3 P.M.
Dinner:	Every day, 3–11 P.M.

Atmosphere/setting: Beautifully done bistro with a bar to the left as you walk in and a large, high-ceilinged room decorated with imagery from ancient and modern Italy. There's a small street-side seating area.

House specialties: Romano-crusted chicken breast; veal piccata; lasagna al forno; roasted portobello mushrooms; frozen Sfuzzi drink.

Other recommendations: Linguine pescatore; sautéed prawns with asparagus; grilled salmon and spinach salad; baked eggplant.

Entertainment & amenities: Catering party and business lunches, wine dinners monthly, sunset menu daily 3–6:30 P.M.

Summary & comments: Part of the national chain, Sfuzzi (pronounced "foozie") is especially popular among young professionals. Food flavors, preparation, and presentation are very modern, though not pushing any envelopes. Prices have come down considerably since the Italian competition in the Gaslamp grew so enormously. Sunday brunch, at around $15 a person, is a good deal.

Honors & awards: *San Diego Magazine,* Best New Restaurant 1992.

Shien of Osaka

	Japanese
	★★★
Zone 1 North County Inland	Inexpensive
16769 Bernardo Center Drive, Suite 11	
451-0074	Quality 85 Value B

Reservations:	Recommended
When to go:	Any time
Entree range:	$7–16
Payment:	VISA, MC, AMEX
Service rating:	★★
Friendliness rating:	★★
Parking:	Free lot
Bar:	Limited
Wine selection:	House
Dress:	Informal
Disabled access:	Yes
Customers:	Locals
Lunch:	Monday–Friday, 11:30 A.M.–2 P.M.;
	Saturday and Sunday, closed.
Dinner:	Monday–Saturday, 5–9:30 P.M.; Sunday, closed.

Atmosphere / setting: A sushi bar occupies an entire wall of this pleasant suburban-looking Japanese restaurant. Opposite the bar are several rows of tables covered with pink tablecloths and glass tops over that. The look is informal and casual.

House specialties: Assorted sushi and sashimi; teriyaki chicken; broiled fish; udon with chicken, shrimp, and vegetable tempura; combination plates.

Other recommendations: Mushroom with grated radish; yams with tuna; potatoes with sliced beef; spinach; fried tofu.

Summary & comments: Shien floats in the mid-space somewhere between the fast and casual attitudes of a noodle house and the comforts of a dinner restaurant. Biggest draws are the sushi bar with its flamboyant chef (and downtown pricing), and the long list of combination plates which team several elements, ample portions, and reasonable prices. The appeal is a broad one since the standard crowd includes members of the dating set, young marrieds, and seniors in search of inexpensive dining.

Solunto Baking Company

	Bakery Cafe
	★★
	Inexpensive
	Quality 78 Value B

Zone 6   Downtown/Uptown/Central
1643 India Street
233-3506

Reservations:	Not accepted
When to go:	Any time
Entree range:	$3–5
Payment:	Cash only
Service rating:	★★
Friendliness rating:	★
Parking:	Street
Bar:	None
Wine selection:	None
Dress:	Informal
Disabled access:	Yes
Customers:	Locals
Open:	Monday–Friday, 7 A.M.–6 P.M.;
	Saturday, 7 A.M.–5 P.M.; Sunday, closed.

Atmosphere/setting: It's an old-fashioned-looking deli and bakery, with the "old" part entirely genuine, since it's been in this location for decades.

House specialties: Eggplant parmigiana; peppers and eggs; sandwiches.

Summary & comments: There was a time when the only alternative to the dominance of fluff 'n fold, overly aerated white bread in San Diego was to be found at Solunto's. Their semolina bread was impeccable, toothsome, and robust; it still is. The sandwiches you get here are tasty enough, but mostly because they come on Solunto's breads and rolls. The variety isn't extraordinary and the flavors are not fashionable, but the taste is solid and satisfying.

SORRENTINO'S
RISTORANTE ITALIANO

Zone 4   Mission Valley and the Mesas
4724 Clairemont Mesa Boulevard
483-1811

Italian	
★ ★ ★	
Inexpensive / Moderate	
Quality 88	Value B

Reservations:	Accepted
When to go:	Dinner
Entree range:	$7–15
Payment:	VISA, MC
Service rating:	★ ★
Friendliness rating:	★ ★ ★
Parking:	Free lot
Bar:	Limited
Wine selection:	House
Dress:	Dressy casual, informal
Disabled access:	Yes
Customers:	Locals
Lunch:	Monday–Friday, 11:30 A.M.–2:30 P.M.; Saturday and Sunday, closed.
Dinner:	Monday–Friday, 5–10 P.M.; Saturday, 5–11 P.M.; Sunday, closed.

Atmosphere / setting: Neighborhood dining room in a shopping-center setting; informal; mid-level lighting.

House specialties: Soups; pizza; homemade cheese-stuffed tortellini with porcini sauce; calzone stuffed with Gorgonzola, ricotta, sun-dried tomatoes, and pine nuts; shrimp with oregano.

Other recommendations: Rigatoni in a spicy marinara sauce; eggplant parmigiana.

Summary & comments: Though not exactly a throwback to the old days of spaghetti-and-meatballs Italian, Sorrentino's has more to do with the old ways than the new ones. It's akin to a neighborhood restaurant in Italy where they're willing to cook food the way you'd like. If you want chicken rather than fish with the lemon caper sauce, that's no problem. If you want your broccoli steamed rather than sautéed, that's okay too. Sauces are terrific, though there's a tendency to overdo it. Modest wine gets served in clunky glasses, but that speaks to the emphatic nature of the place.

Souplantation

★★★★
Inexpensive

Quality 90   Value A

Zone 1   North County Inland
17210 Bernardo Center Drive,
   Rancho Bernardo
675-3353

Zone 2   North County Coastal
1860 Marron Road, Carlsbad
434-9100

Zone 7   San Diego East/East County
9158 Fletcher Parkway, La Mesa
462-4232

Reservations:	Not accepted
When to go:	Any time
Entree range:	Lunch, $5; dinner, $7
Payment:	VISA, MC, D
Service rating:	★★★
Friendliness rating:	★★★★★
Parking:	Free lot
Bar:	Limited
Wine selection:	Limited
Dress:	Informal
Disabled access:	Yes
Customers:	Locals
Open:	Sunday–Thursday, 11 A.M.–9 P.M.;
	Friday and Saturday, 11 A.M.–10 P.M.

Atmosphere/setting: It's a soup-and-salad cafeteria and looks like one. The older Souplantations tend to look a little scruffy, but the newer ones are spotlessly modern, filled with booths and tables, and decorated in a homey fashion.

House specialties: Crisp fresh salad ingredients; mixed green salads; pasta salads; chicken soup; black bean chili; baked potato; low-fat frozen yogurt.

Summary & comments: There are many Souplantations in the region, and at all of them one price covers everything, and you can go back for seconds as often as you'd like. Souplantation combines your great aunt's obsession with cleanliness, your adolescent son's concern with quantity, and a food critic's worry over freshness and palatability. It's not just lettuce and tomatoes and shredded jicama that draw crowds here, it's also the five kinds of soups, the array of pastas and sauces, the potatoes, the breads and muffins, the dessert bar . . . and the prices. This is a place of great down-to-earth values, a wholesome and happy meeting ground of the generations. Check the phone book for other locations.

Sportsmen's Seafood

Zone 5   Mission Bay and Beaches
1617 Quivera Road
224-3551

Seafood	
★	
Inexpensive	
Quality 60	Value D

Reservations:	Not accepted
When to go:	Lunchtime
Entree range:	$2–7
Payment:	VISA, MC, D
Service rating:	★
Friendliness rating:	★
Parking:	Free lot
Bar:	Limited
Wine selection:	None
Dress:	Informal
Disabled access:	Yes
Customers:	Locals
Open:	Monday, 11 A.M.–4 P.M.;
	Tuesday–Thursday, 11 A.M.–7 P.M.;
	Friday and Saturday, 11 A.M.–8 P.M.;
	Sunday, 11 A.M.–7:30 P.M.
	(closing times vary with daylight)

Atmosphere / setting: Inside the ambience is strictly that of an elderly and dark coffee shop, one that's seen better times. There's a window where you place your order and a scattering of formica-topped tables and squeaky chairs where you can wait until they call your number. Outside—which is where you want to be—there are concrete tables and benches.

House specialties: Ceviche; fish and chips; fried clams.

Summary & comments: What's special about Sportsmen's Seafood is not most of the seafood, though the octopus ceviche is very good and the sandwich of fried clams is digestible enough. The reason to be here is the setting. When you sit on the patio outside, the water is no more than 20 feet away. Right in front of you boats bob up and down, gulls swoop, and if the sun is shining (it most often is), you'll feel like there's no better place on earth.

Sushi Deli

Japanese / Sushi Bar

★★

Inexpensive

Quality 76   Value B

Zone 6   Downtown / Uptown / Central
828 Broadway
231-9597

Zone 6   Downtown / Uptown / Central
339 West Broadway
233-3072

Reservations:	Not accepted
When to go:	Lunch
Entree range:·	$4–13
Payment:	VISA, MC
Service rating:	★★
Friendliness rating:	★★
Parking:	Street
Bar:	Limited
Wine selection:	House
Dress:	Informal
Disabled access:	Yes
Customers:	Locals, businesspeople
Lunch:	Monday–Friday, 11:30 A.M.–2 P.M.;
	Saturday and Sunday, closed.
Dinner:	Monday–Friday, 5–9 P.M.;
	Saturday, 5–10 P.M.; Sunday, closed.

Atmosphere / setting: At 828 Broadway you'll find a squarish storefront with a big glass window in front and a series of nondescript tables and chairs. It looks like a lunchroom. The 329 West Broadway location is in a hotel and looks like a coffee shop.

House specialties: Sushi combos; sashimi tei sho ku; steamed gyoza; chicken cutlet; pork curry; seafood tempura; vegetable udon; shrimp ramen.

Other recommendations: Catfish tempura; tofu salad; sesame chicken; teriyaki chicken; tempura udon.

Summary & comments: The Sushi Deli provides lots of good, though not extraordinary, sushi. What makes it notable are the modest prices. The Sushi Deli at 828 Broadway also happens to be the darling of local designers and architects who flock there at lunchtime. Japanese food other than sushi is available, but at the 339 West Broadway location (known as Sushi Deli Too), much of it tastes like it was prepared in haste. If you have the option, the original location at 828 Broadway is the better choice.

Sushi Ota

	Japanese / Sushi Bar
	★★★
	Moderate
	Quality 88 Value D

Zone 5   Mission Bay and Beaches
4529 Mission Bay Drive
270-5670

Reservations:	Recommended
When to go:	Dinner
Entree range:	$8–20
Payment:	VISA, MC
Service rating:	★★
Friendliness rating:	★
Parking:	Free lot
Bar:	Limited
Wine selection:	House
Dress:	Dressy casual, informal
Disabled access:	Yes
Customers:	Locals, ethnic
Lunch:	Tuesday–Friday, 11:30 A.M.–2 P.M.; Saturday–Monday, closed.
Dinner:	Every day, 5:30–10:30 P.M.

Atmosphere / setting: The restaurant might be a little hard to find since it's set in the far corner of a small shopping center. The interior of the restaurant is done in an austere manner, with black tables and chairs and grey walls. The sushi bar is to the right as you walk in.

House specialties: Sushi is the big draw, both at the small sushi bar and among the diners at the tables. The selection is extensive and unusual.

Other recommendations: Baked beef with asparagus; grilled yellow tail; gyoza; fried soft-shell crabs; chicken teriyaki; tempura.

Summary & comments: Though the location is not the most convenient, San Diegans beat a daily path to the door of Sushi Ota. The reason is indisputably the very fresh sushi served in interesting and attractive presentations. When you sit at a table, you are handed a list of more than 40 different types of sushi and a small pencil, and you mark how much you want of each item. There's also a regular Japanese menu if you want to order non-sushi items, and about 25% of diners opt to do so. Much of the clientele is Japanese and known by name by restaurant personnel.

Thai Chada

Zone 5   Mission Bay and Beaches
1749 Garnet Avenue
270-1888

Reservations:	Recommended
When to go:	Dinner
Entree range:	$7–13
Payment:	VISA, MC, AMEX, DC, D
Service rating:	★★
Friendliness rating:	★★
Parking:	Street
Bar:	Limited
Wine selection:	House
Dress:	Informal
Disabled access:	Yes
Customers:	Locals
Lunch:	Monday–Friday, 11:30 A.M.–2:30 P.M.; Saturday and Sunday, closed.
Dinner:	Sunday–Thursday, 5–10 P.M.; Friday and Saturday, 5–10:30 P.M.

Atmosphere / setting: The restaurant is one large square room in which the decor—glass-topped tables and several wall hangings—is more serviceable than warm.

House specialties: Pad thai; squash with eggplant and basil; shrimp and broccoli; spicy duck with burnt chile paste.

Other recommendations: Shrimp with bean thread; deep-fried whole fish served with sautéed garlic; scallops with basil; stir-fry squid with string beans; beef Panang curry.

Summary & comments: The menu of some 300 items appears overwhelming at first, but a little inspection reveals a cross-indexer at work: Many of the same dishes appear under more than one heading, although sometimes there's a slight variation. Still, the variety is truly considerable and so are the flavors. The stars on the menu which are supposed to indicate degree of heat are totally unreliable, so tell your server exactly how spicy you want your dishes, regardless of the rating.

Honors & awards: *San Diego Home / Garden Magazine,* Silver Fork Award; *San Diego Magazine,* Critics' Choice 1990.

Thee Bungalow

	Continental
	★★★
	Moderate
	Quality 88 Value B

Zone 5   Mission Bay and Beaches
4996 West Point Loma Boulevard
224-2884

Reservations:	Recommended
When to go:	Any time
Entree range:	$10–22
Payment:	VISA, MC, AMEX, DC, D
Service rating:	★★★
Friendliness rating:	★★★
Parking:	Street, free lot
Bar:	Limited
Wine selection:	Extensive
Dress:	Dressy casual
Disabled access:	Yes
Customers:	Locals
Dinner:	Monday–Thursday, 5:30–9:30 P.M.;
	Friday and Saturday, 5–10 P.M.;
	Sunday, 5–9 P.M.

Atmosphere / setting: A charming little bungalow, complete with fireplace, beamed ceiling, and a strong sense of homeyness. It's been around for quite a long time, so don't be surprised if you see literal fraying around the edges.

House specialties: Roast duck; rack of lamb; house-cured salmon; escargot bourguignon; osso bungalow.

Other recommendations: Veal sweetbreads; crab cakes.

Summary & comments: A quaint, family-run business, Thee Bungalow is a romantic cottage where the meals tend to be surprisingly hearty. Duck is always done well. Call in advance to see if they're running any of their dining specials that provide full meals for around $11; sometimes you have to be there before 6 P.M. to take advantage of them.

Top o' the Cove

Zone 3   La Jolla
1216 Prospect Street
454-7779

Continental
★★★★
Expensive

Quality 93   Value C

Reservations:	Recommended
When to go:	Any time
Entree range:	$24–29
Payment:	VISA, MC, AMEX, DC
Service rating:	★★★★
Friendliness rating:	★★
Parking:	Free lot, street, valet in the evening
Bar:	Full service
Wine selection:	Extensive
Dress:	Dressy
Disabled access:	Yes
Customers:	Locals, businesspeople, visitors/tourists
Brunch:	Every day, 10:30 A.M.–2:30 P.M.
Lunch:	Every day, 11:30 A.M.–2:30 P.M.
Dinner:	Every day, 5:30–10:30 P.M.
	Cafe: 10:30 P.M.–midnight

Atmosphere/setting: Moody, romantic, and elegant, Top o' the Cove is a series of rooms that narrow as you move forward; it concludes in a small, cozy enclave that seems to be hanging over the water.

House specialties: Medallions of smoked salmon with crème fraîche; duck with arugula; roast elk with pinot noir sauce; muscovy duck with Armagnac and walnut sauce; fettuccine with shrimp and scallops.

Other recommendations: Veal piccata; filet with bacon and pearl onions; roasted chicken with rosemary and tomatoes; ravioli of bison and goat cheese.

Entertainment & amenities: Piano player on Wednesday through Sunday evenings.

Summary & comments: An old-fashioned holdout in a modern era—and one of the few truly important continental restaurants left in town—Top o' the Cove has an updated menu, a fabulous view of La Jolla Cove (if you make your reservation for a window table early), comfortably elegant service, and an inspired wine list. Long the restaurant of choice for marriage proposals, anniversaries, prom night, or just because you're special, the sense of elegance and romance hangs heavy. And for very special occasions, there's also one particular booth that's so private it's virtually a room of its own.

Honors & awards: *Wine Spectator* Grand Award; *San Diego Magazine,* Most Romantic.

TRATTORIA ACQUA

	Italian/Mediterranean
Zone 3 La Jolla	★★★★
1298 Prospect Street	Moderate
454-0709	
	Quality 90 Value C

Reservations:	Recommended
When to go:	Any time
Entree range:	$9–19
Payment:	VISA, MC, AMEX
Service rating:	★★★
Friendliness rating:	★★★
Parking:	Free lot with two hours validated, valet, street
Bar:	Full service
Wine selection:	Extensive
Dress:	Dressy casual
Disabled access:	Yes
Customers:	Locals, visitors/tourists
Brunch:	Saturday and Sunday, 11:30 A.M.–3 P.M.
Lunch:	Monday–Friday, 11:30 A.M.–3 P.M.
Dinner:	Sunday–Thursday, 5–10 P.M.;
	Friday and Saturday, 5–11 P.M.

Atmosphere/setting: There are exposed woods and sweeps of bare wall punctuated with romantic renderings of cherubs and an occasional trompe l'oeil. They give the rooms—of which there are several, plus an outdoor courtyard—as much a sense of country French (which the restaurant last occupying these premises was) as it does Italian.

House specialties: Herb-roasted chicken with barley risotto; braised lamb shank; osso buco; fresh pastas; seasonal menu changes every three months.

Other recommendations: Seafood stew with couscous; roasted pork tenderloin with grilled apples; pizza with pesto and roasted chicken.

Entertainment & amenities: Ocean view (limited), outside seating.

Summary & comments: Unlike many local Italian restaurants that have an urgency about them, Trattoria Acqua has a different metabolism. It's not a place of splash or high drama. Rather, it's quieter, calmer, and full of little surprises. The menu is large and interesting. Eggplant stuffed with goat cheese and served on a bed of marinara is creamy and delicious. Fried calamari is awfully good, as is the osso buco, which comes atop a dynamite barley risotto. All pasta is available in full and half portions. Desserts are worth the calories.

Honors & awards: San Diego Restaurant Association, Best New Restaurant; *Travel Holiday,* Top 300 Restaurants in America; *Epicurean Rendezvous,* Top 100 Restaurants in Southern California.

TRATTORIA MANNINO

	Italian / Sicilian
Zone 3 La Jolla	★★★
5662 La Jolla Boulevard	Inexpensive / Moderate
551-8610	
	Quality 83 Value B

Reservations:	Recommended
When to go:	Any time
Entree range:	$8–15
Payment:	VISA, MC, AMEX, D
Service rating:	★★
Friendliness rating:	★★★
Parking:	Free lot, street
Bar:	Full service
Wine selection:	Good
Dress:	Dressy casual
Disabled access:	Yes
Customers:	Locals
Dinner:	Every day, 5–10 P.M.

Atmosphere / setting: An odd interior arrangement left over from a previous tenant results in a modern-looking divider separating the restaurant into two unequal parts: a narrow area in front fits three tables, and then a deeper space in back has about a dozen more. Dark-stained wood paneling lines the walls, plants are scattered around, and the large red tiles on the floor give Mannino's a cool urban sophistication.

House specialties: Pasta is a specialty with over 20 to choose from, all made to order, most made in-house: rigatoni with ricotta and eggplant; farfalle with salmon, peas, and vodka; capellini with scallops and sun-dried tomatoes.

Other recommendations: Sea bass in a spicy tomato sauce; veal scaloppine with artichokes; veal stuffed with prosciutto and provolone; gnocchi with tomato and radicchio; veal and mushroom ravioli in a mascarpone sauce.

Summary & comments: Something of a sleeper, this family-run operation often seems to have more people in the kitchen than out front. But contrary to the old saw, too many cooks only seem to enhance the final product at Mannino's. Sauces are often quite unusual, and so is the pairing of ingredients. Fish is handled well, especially the sea bass which turns out bold and meaty—not the meek and wispy dish it so commonly is. Risottos are phenomenal. Portions are large, and it all seems like the very definition of comfort food.

Honors & awards: *San Diego Home / Garden Magazine* Readers' Poll, Best Italian.

UNIVERSITY Club

	American
	★★★★
	Moderate/Expensive
	Quality 94 Value C

Zone 6   Downtown/Uptown/Central
Symphony Tower, 750 B Street
234-5200

Reservations:	Can be made by members only
When to go:	Any time
Entree range:	Lunch, $9–18; dinner, $19–30
Payment:	VISA, MC
Service rating:	★★★★
Friendliness rating:	★★★
Parking:	Fee lot
Bar:	Full service
Wine selection:	Good
Dress:	Business attire
Disabled access:	Yes
Customers:	Businesspeople
Open:	Monday–Friday, 7 A.M.–11 P.M.;
	Saturday, 5–11 P.M.; Sunday, closed.

Atmosphere/setting: Richly but oh-so-discreetly appointed, with lush carpeting, crisp white napery, widely spaced tables, and wonderful views of downtown San Diego provided via a wall of windows that wrap three sides of the dining room.

House specialties: Stilton-crusted rack of lamb; mustard-baked salmon; New York steak; seared scallops; vegetarian risotto; mahimahi.

Other recommendations: Dover sole; veal chops; Gorgonzola ravioli; grilled swordfish.

Summary & comments: Though the University Club is a private dining room, fortunately many merely moderately connected folks belong—especially if they happen to be associated with a local law firm. The University Club shares with the sitcom *Cheers* the fact that the hostess and maître d' will greet members by name as soon as they enter the lobby area. It is a perfect spot for business meals and power brokering, and it also serves elegant, well-conceived meals that combine fashion and substance. When you say "rare" or "lightly dressed," there's never a need to say it twice. The menu changes daily. Also, money is never in evidence at the University Club; members sign a bill that covers everyone at the table.

Vigilucci's Trattoria Italiana

Zone 2 North County Coastal	Italian
506 First Street, Encinitas	★★★
942-7332	Inexpensive/Moderate
	Quality 85 Value B

Reservations:	Only for 4 or more
When to go:	Any time
Entree range:	$6–15
Payment:	VISA, MC, AMEX, DC, D
Service rating:	★★★
Friendliness rating:	★★
Parking:	Street
Bar:	Limited
Wine selection:	Good
Dress:	Informal
Disabled access:	Yes
Customers:	Locals
Lunch:	Monday–Friday, 11 A.M.–3 P.M.;
	Saturday and Sunday, closed.
Dinner:	Monday–Thursday, 5–10 P.M.;
	Friday and Saturday, 5–10:30 P.M.;
	Sunday, 3–10 P.M.

Atmosphere/setting: A pleasant storefront restaurant on the main street of Encinitas, Vigilucci's has a low ceiling and lots of closely spaced tables which, though covered with white tablecloths, are topped with glass and set with a small vase of fresh flowers. Against the back wall is a bar where diners stand and wait for tables to free up.

House specialties: Pasta: angelhair with garlic, bacon, and fresh vegetables; linguine with seafood; penne with black olives and capers; lasagna.

Other recommendations: Chicken breast breaded, fried, and served with lemon wedges; veal stuffed with prosciutto; grilled calamari; mixed seafood grill.

Summary & comments: A local phenomenon, Vigilucci's is typically mobbed shortly after it opens for business each day. The big draw is excellent pasta employed in tasty, well-prepared traditional Italian dishes that use very fresh ingredients, are served in large portions, and are priced astonishingly well: most entrees are under $10. Don't miss the mixed antipasto which should be shared by two and might be enough dinner for a light eater.

Wazwan Indian Cuisine

	Indian
	★★★
	Inexpensive
	Quality 80 Value B

Zone 1   North County Inland
North County Fair Food Court,
   200 East Via Rancho Parkway,
   Escondido
743-1116

Zone 4   Mission Valley and the Mesas
University Towne Center Food Court,
   4545 La Jolla Village Drive
552-8300

Reservations:	Not accepted
When to go:	Any time
Entree range:	$4–6
Payment:	Cash only
Service rating:	★★
Friendliness rating:	★★★
Parking:	Free lot
Bar:	None
Wine selection:	None
Dress:	Informal
Disabled access:	Yes
Customers:	Locals, visitors/tourists
Open:	Monday–Friday, 10 A.M.–9 P.M.;
	Saturday, 10 A.M.–8 P.M.; Sunday, 11 A.M.–6 P.M.

Atmosphere/setting: Whatever atmosphere exists is borrowed from the shopping center food court where it's located.

House specialties: Lamb curry; vegetarian samosas; honey-lemon chicken; spinach and dal curry; onion paratha (onion-stuffed bread).

Summary & comments: The integration of Indian food into local shopping centers brings the wonders of just-baked naan and a host of stews, curries, and kebabs to weary shoppers. It's important to ask for samples of what looks good, because flavorings and the intensity of seasonings tend to change from one time and location to another.

WineSellar and Brasserie

	French
	★★★★
	Moderate/Expensive
	Quality 93 Value C

Zone 4   Mission Valley and the Mesas
9550 Waples Street, Suite 115
450-9576

Reservations:	Recommended
When to go:	Any time
Entree range:	$16–25
Payment:	VISA, MC, AMEX, DC, D
Service rating:	★★
Friendliness rating:	★★
Parking:	Free lot
Bar:	Limited
Wine selection:	Extensive
Dress:	Business attire, dressy casual
Disabled access:	No
Customers:	Locals, businesspeople
Lunch:	Saturday, 11:30 A.M.–2 P.M.; Sunday–Friday, closed.
Dinner:	Tuesday–Saturday, 5:30–10 P.M.; Sunday and Monday, closed.

Atmosphere/setting: A medium-sized room that you can take in with a single glance. It's smartly done in bleached and blond oak, with brightly uphol-stered chairs and banquettes and strong simple lines. A happy bistro.

House specialties: Menu changes seasonally. Depending on chance and the time of year, Algerian salad, roasted eggplant soup, and rabbit may be available. Escolar is sensational.

Summary & comments: Though it's a bit hard to find—even though you can see it from the street—the Brasserie is an oasis of good taste in a quasi-industrial office-park setting. Once located, you've still got to pass through the downstairs wine shop to get to the upstairs restaurant. The menu is eclectic and seasonal with a French accent, all of it produced by an owner/chef with a his-tory of astonishing kitchen wizardry. Fish is particularly well and knowledgeably treated. The Brasserie is also a good place to arrange small, special-occasion din-ners where menus can be individually tailored and the success of the wine pair-ings is virtually guaranteed.

Honors & awards: *Wine Spectator* Grand Award for one of the best 100 wines in the world, 1989 to present; *Travel and Leisure,* one of the 50 best restau-rants in the country.

ZINC CAFE

Zone 2   North County Coastal
132 South Cedros Avenue, Solana Beach
793-5436

American	
★★★	
Inexpensive	
Quality 88	Value C

Reservations:	Not accepted
When to go:	Any time
Entree range:	$4–7
Payment:	Cash
Service rating:	★★
Friendliness rating:	★★
Parking:	Free lot
Bar:	None
Wine selection:	None
Dress:	Informal
Disabled access:	Yes
Customers:	Locals
Open:	Monday, 7 A.M.–noon;
	Tuesday–Saturday, 7 A.M.–5:30 P.M.;
	Sunday, 7 A.M.–5 P.M.

Atmosphere / setting: Zinc's is a tiny little box, sparingly and artfully decorated, with a counter and a few chairs. The look is distinctly Crate and Barrel. There's a small outdoor patio that radiates charm.

House specialties: Oatmeal with sour cherries; frittata with salsa; pizza with chiles, tomato, and smoked Gouda; black bean chili; Zinc Burger.

Other recommendations: Pizza with garlic, chard, mozzarella, and goat cheese; daily soup; desserts.

Summary & comments: For several blocks in either direction of Zinc's there are many shops featuring arts and fine handicrafts. Zinc's fits into the setting perfectly, with its limited but very sophisticated menu of snacks and light meals. Folks behind the counter tend to be kindly but inexperienced, so there's sometimes a little disorganization that accompanies the service. But it all seems to end well if you just have patience.

Eclectic Gourmet Guide to San Diego
Reader Survey

If you would like to express your opinion about your San Diego dining experiences or this guidebook, complete the following survey and mail it to:

Eclectic Gourmet Guide Reader Survey
P.O. Box 43059
Birmingham, AL 35243

	Diner 1	Diner 2	Diner 3	Diner 4	Diner 5
Gender (M or F)	_____	_____	_____	_____	_____
Age	_____	_____	_____	_____	_____
Hometown	_____	_____	_____	_____	_____

Tell us about the restaurants you've visited . . . .

Your overall experience:

Restaurant	👍	👎
_____	_____	_____
_____	_____	_____
_____	_____	_____
_____	_____	_____
_____	_____	_____
_____	_____	_____
_____	_____	_____

Comments you'd like to share with other diners:

_____
_____
_____
_____
_____
_____
_____
_____
_____
_____